Does The

OWL

Still Call
Your Name?

Does The OWL Still Call Your Name?

PATHS OF STRUGGLE AND RENEWAL

Edited by Bruce Brand

INDIAN

LIFE BOOKS

DOES THE OWL STILL CALL YOUR NAME?
Paths of Struggle and Renewal
Edited by Bruce Brand

Published by Indian Life Books
A Division of Indian Life Ministries

ISBN 0-920379-18-4

First published July 2000, Fourth printing 2014
© 2000 Indian Life Ministries

Cover and interior design by Uttley/DouPonce DesignWorks,
Sisters, Oregon, www.uddesignworks.com

Unless otherwise marked, all Scripture quotations are from
Holy Bible, *New Life Bible* (NLB), published by
Christian Literature International, Canby, OR 97013.
© 1969, 1976, 1978, 1983, 1986.

Printed and bound in Canada.

Visit Indian Life Ministries' website at www.indianlife.org

00 01 02 03 04 05   10 9 8 7 6 5 4 3 2 1

To all those who have heard the owl call their name,
but have chosen instead to follow another call.
The call of the One greater than themselves who has
set them free and transformed their lives.

Table of Contents

Preface

As one looks out across the landscape of Native North America, there are two ways to look at what one sees. It is possible to look at the scenery and see only barrenness and destruction. On the other hand, we can see past the destruction—grim statistics, the pain, oppression and darkness—and find hope. Hope that people can change; hope that things don't have to stay the same and even get worse.

Margaret Craven wrote a book entitled *I Heard the Owl Call My Name*. Her fictional account tells the story of a young minister who was sent by his bishop to a remote Native American community. The bishop sent him on a mission—to find God during his time there. You see, the bishop knew that this man had only a short time to live. He wanted him to discover God for himself while he still had time. During the minister's time there, he heard the owl call his name.

As is common in many Native traditions, the owl is an ominous sign—usually of bad luck or death. Some are not only very fearful of owls, they have had personal encounters with them.

Pete Grey Eyes, a medicine man, tells of having owls appear in the juniper trees outside his hogan. There was not only one but several. They would come out and hoot throughout the night.

Pete says "These owls began to talk to me in a Navajo way. They would say, 'We are going to kill you...you...you! We are going to kill you!'"

As a man who practiced Native medicine and was in touch with the spirit world, Pete knew that these owls weren't speaking to him themselves. "They were demons sent by another medicine man to an owl. When a medicine man makes contact with the spirit world, these spirits are given to him to help him in his dealing in witchcraft."

Pete says, "I tried all my powers to get rid of these owls and stop my livestock from dying and to heal my family, but nothing changed. It was no use!"

Addictions like gambling, alcohol, pornography, and sexual addictions bind many people. Some are so distraught they have tried to commit suicide in an attempt to break free from the chains that bind them. For many they hear the owl calling their name and they are living in fear—certainty that they can't change and they are dying a slow, painful death.

They are like the psalmist who wrote, "I am like an owl of the waste places. I lie awake. And I feel like a bird alone on the roof. Those who hate me [my enemies—my addictions] have made it hard for me all day long. Those who are angry with me curse my name" (Psalm 102:6-8 NLB).

Does the Owl Still Call Your Name? is written for those who have heard that there is hope and maybe even have tried to do something about it. Perhaps they've even turned their lives over to God the Creator, and asked Him, through His Son Jesus to heal their brokenness, yet they still hear that old owl calling their name.

God says that we don't need to live in fear of the owls in our lives—our enemies who threaten evil. He wants us to be like the eagle and to soar on eagles' wings.

You can read Pete Grey Eyes' story (page 327) of how he found freedom and chased those owls out of his life.

This book is formed around articles that previously appeared in *Indian Life* newspaper. It addresses issues that are serious social concerns of the Native people of North America. The text is arranged to deal with one of the concerns in each section.

Individuals who have experienced long and deep struggles with addiction or disease tell the personal stories written in this book. Some had their battles because of decisions made by the individual; others battled demons that were not of their own making. Some of the personal stories were gained by means of interview. All were given willingly with the prayer that the revelation of the person's confused thinking, defeats and, in most cases, eventual winning of the battle, will bring insight and help to readers.

Words are powerful tools, which can hurt or heal. It is with the prayer for the healing of many who are suffering that this book is published.

—Bruce Brand and Jim Uttley

CHAPTER ONE

Does Alcohol Still Call
Your Name?

ALCOHOL AND THE LAW
by John Foote

Of all the threats to the peace, security and well-being of the Indian since contact with white people, none has been worse than the introduction of alcoholic beverages. Although law forbade the sale of liquor to Aboriginals, in 1832 many white traders were unable to resist the chance to get rich. Though it was illegal for Indians to possess liquor until 1953, drinking among the Indians greatly increased during the 1930s when they became deeply discouraged over worsening conditions brought about by the Great Depression. In addition, the Indians were also greatly distressed over the failure of the governmental programs that were supposed to be helping them.

Since alcohol had traditionally been foreign to the Indian culture, their bodies had no opportunity whatever to develop a tolerance for this new drug. When the Indian first started drinking the results often were ruin and destruction for him. The older people tried hard to keep the younger ones away from the whiskey. It was impossible. The young people would come home drunk and cause trouble.

Despite the fact that almost all tribes have since voted against liquor on the reservation, this has not stopped drinking and it never will. On most reservations the tribal councils have prohibited the sale of liquor for many years but liquor may be brought into the reservation from the outside. There is usually just as much drinking off the reservation as on.

Aboriginals are often ignorant of the law and their rights under it. As a result they are frequently arrested on drunkenness charges simply because they do their drinking in public taverns or bars where the public and the police can see them, instead of at home or in restaurants like many non-Aboriginals do. There is also much lack of communication and understanding between these Indians and the law enforcement officers. For instance, there are a number of Indians who are classified as "homeless alcoholics" who are sentenced with the hope that in custody they will obtain needed care, food and shelter. There is also the fact that most Indians cannot afford the services of a lawyer.

Far too many Indians, over 7.5 percent of the entire Indian population, get into trouble with the police. For example, in Minnesota, Indian people make up only .006 percent of the total population of the state yet they make up 8 percent of the adult inmates in state correctional facilities. In many cases the crimes are minor ones such as drunkenness, disorderly conduct, vagrancy, simple assault, and traffic offenses. Many of these offenders simply are sentenced to the local workhouse where the Indian population ranges from 10 to 33 percent of the total. Not taking repeaters into account, Indians have made up about one-third of the referrals to Minnesota's Hennepin County Municipal Court Probation Office.

A major problem of the courts in dealing with Indians is the fact that the courts have never been able to handle the different culture of the Indian. This causes much distrust and ill feeling on the part of the Indians toward the system. This carries over into other areas of Indian-White relations and strengthens negative feelings that work both ways. Thus the problems of the Indian are multiplied.

Native peoples' difficulty with law enforcement officers today can be much better understood if we consider their history and original culture. Before his whole way of life was uprooted and changed by the coming of the Europeans, the Indian had an established and time-tested way of dealing with those who broke the tribal law. In the first place, much crime was prevented and treated by the ancient Indian system of shame, ridicule and shutting the offender off from society. If a crime was committed every tribe had its own police force and the families that were directly involved in the crime took care of the punishment. The offender paid for an offense against another person by making things right with that person. The accused had to face his sentence and was usually willing to pay the price. Few white men ever really understood the Indian system. This is still the major problem between Indians and whites today.

The coming of the white man and the setting up of reservations caused many serious problems for the Aboriginals. Because their own ways were now denied them, their system of law enforcement broke down. This left the Indians very confused. Their basic needs no longer were being met and they lost their strong pride and self-reliance. Instead, they now were confronted with a new and strange system, which they neither wanted nor understood. When alcohol was introduced to them this strange drug then became their escape from very unhappy circumstances. Alcohol became a common drink and brought with it more ugly problems.

There is a solution to all these problems.

As one example I want to tell you a little about my brother. For many years he was an alcoholic. His condition seemed to be utterly hopeless. Time after time he would get drunk and his drunkenness would cause much trouble and very anxious times for all of us. This went on year after year. We tried to do everything in our power to help him but it was no use. It actually seemed that he was living in jails and in other public institutions more than he was living at home. The most pitiful part of it was that he became completely helpless to help himself.

Finally, one day, our wonderful Lord stepped in by arranging circumstances as He so often does. My family for various reasons found it necessary to move away from Minneapolis. At the time this seemed to be cruel. It left my poor brother alone to face his condition and all the problems it brought to him: praise God, he was not alone! Finding no relative to lean upon in the most desperate moment of his life he cried out to the only Person in all the universe who could possibly help him and He did. My brother was completely healed of alcoholism. Today he is a successful interior decorator and has been for years.

What about you? Our God and Lord can do the same for you no matter what your present situation is or how low you may have sunk. Like my brother you may have considered suicide. You might be considering it right now. Don't do it. There is no reason for you to go down into everlasting defeat when there is help available. Jesus Christ can meet your need as He met my brother's.

ON THE LOOKOUT
by *William Dumas*

For the past hour and one-half I have watched one of my Indian brothers sitting across the street on a windowsill and, from where I sit, I can see that he has had a bit to drink.

I have been asking myself, "What is a man of his age doing sitting on a window sill?"

He looks to be about fifty but I could be wrong. (Booze can really age a person.) He is a short man with shabby clothes and a sharp-peaked cap still commonly used by our brothers his age. What strikes me more is that he reminds me so much of a vulture. Maybe it is because of his cap and the way he is holding his hands. His head constantly darts back and forth searching up and down the street for someone who will bring the next drink and I pray that nobody ever shows up.

Every once in a while someone will share the windowsill with him, not for his company but for a place to survey the scene. Then they will spy a likely prospect and slowly walk on over to beg or bully the victim for a drink in the bar. Along the street there are other groups doing the same thing, staring thirstily towards the hotel, waiting for someone to come along so they can quench the thirst that only the drinking man knows.

Someone must have received enough money to buy a bottle because a little group has disappeared behind a building to make quick work of the contents, the way a thirsty man gulps down a glass of cold water on a hot day. Boosted by the spirits in the bottle they will come out more boldly and aggressively to beg for the nickels and quarters needed to buy the next one. After a few more trips behind the building they will forget who they are. Then they will wander around town being abusive to others and especially to themselves. They will tire shortly, walking around blindly and with an empty stomach and will try to make it home. They will be back in the morning long before the bar is opened to start the only thing they care for now: begging for coins for that first drink of the day or to buy a bottle to take behind the buildings.

Yes, my brothers, we are in real bad shape and we must face the fact that we are up to our necks in alcohol and some of our brothers are drowning. We must swim to shore where there is safety and make a light so our brothers can see to escape.

There are a lot of reasons for the condition so many of our brothers are in, but let's not say it is their problem; it is ours too. It really hurts me to see father, mother and daughter standing together waiting for someone to give them the added problems alcohol brings.

My brother is still sitting on that windowsill. He must be tired for every once in a while his head nods only to be jolted awake by the cold evening air to continue his vigilance. His head continues to move quickly back and forth, up and down the street, as he waits, searching for the drink he craves.

Brother, if you only knew how I feel for you, but there is nothing I can do that will alter the shape you and our people are in. Only the faint hope that I have swum ashore and started a warm fire. You, too, can swim ashore from alcohol and start your fire where it is peaceful and we can all be happy together again.

FRIEND, YOU MUST make a choice between Jesus Christ and alcohol. That's the choice you will have to make. Jesus Christ is the Son of the Living God who died for the sins of His people so that whoever believes in Him will not perish but have everlasting life (John 3:16).

If a person turns to Jesus, confesses his sin, and trusts Him for salvation, Jesus will supply that person with what he needs through the power of His Holy Spirit.

This is why Ephesians 5 says,

> *Don't be drunk with wine, but be filled with the Holy Spirit of Christ.*

Believe in Jesus and you will have the courage you need. You will have the sense of purpose and the joy you are looking for. I'm making this very simple and I know it. There's a lot to what I'm talking about, and I think you should find a church where Jesus is the center in order to find out what all this means. Right now I want to be simple about this. The alternatives are simply put in the Bible: alcohol or Jesus.

I can understand why people who don't know Jesus need alcohol to keep their sanity. Once you know Him He will help you fight the alcohol problem.

What will happen to you if Jesus doesn't help you? You cannot go on the way you are right now, can you?

My advice to you is simple: understand that you

have to make a choice between what alcohol can give you and what Christ can give you. Choose Christ and find life.

Parents, you are going to have to also make a choice. I am fully aware of all the arguments that suggest that you have a perfect right to drink. Let's assume that they are all valid, but even if you do have a right, look what you are doing to yourself and to your children. Honestly now, can you really get through a day without alcohol? Isn't it true that already in the morning you look forward to your first drink? You are drinking at noon, too, aren't you? And in the evening? How many ounces of alcohol a day do you consume? Maybe you can handle this now but what is going to happen if you really come up against a full-blown crisis in your life?

This is a spiritual matter. I invite you to turn to the Lord Jesus Christ and ask Him to substitute the power of His Spirit for the power of alcohol in your life. So much is at stake. Christ can save you from whatever slavery you have fallen into and He can make your life beautiful and meaningful. He can give you resources to face yourself, your problems and your frustrations.

Let's be realistic. Let's not be absurd about this problem. Don't let the enjoyment of the taste of alcohol and the pleasure it gives cloud your mind so that you forget that wine is a mocker. The Bible says it is; you know it is (Proverbs 20:1).

Look at what is at stake. Alcohol can make a fool of you. It can destroy you and the children you love. This is why you need Jesus. Turn to Him and ask for forgiveness and ask for His Spirit.

Alcohol may be too strong for you but the Bible says we can do all things because Christ gives us the strength (Philippians 4:13).

Give Him a chance.

Many Problems, One Result
by Arthur Holmes

A man came into my office one day at one of the counseling centers where I worked. He wanted to talk about the death of his wife. She had been well liked in the neighborhood and well known. As long as she was alive their home was busy with people coming and going. There was always someone visiting.

This man was used to the activity. When his wife died and the funeral was over he thought people would come to see him. They didn't; no one came to talk with him. He had no company.

The hours went by and still he was alone. About ten o'clock in the evening he couldn't take it anymore. He was filled with such anger at the coldness of the people who left him to handle his grief alone that he had to strike back. He put on his jacket, headed down to the liquor store and began drinking. The end result was his eventual commitment to the treatment center where I worked. This man is a good example of what happens when pathological grief is left untreated.

Wise King Solomon asks several questions and then answers them very pointedly in Proverbs 23:29,30. He says

Who has trouble? Who has sorrow? Who is fighting? Who is complaining? Who is hurt without reason? Who has eyes that become red? Those who stay a long time over wine. Those who go to taste mixed wine.

When I look at these verses I see a perfect picture of a grieving person with an alcohol problem: sorrow, weeping and lingering long over wine. The man described at the beginning fits this picture very well. Our emotional and mental components are so closely linked to our physical bodies that when one part is afflicted in some way another part of our being may show the reaction. In the case just stated the rage and hurt this man felt at the neglect of his neighbors resulted in a severe addiction problem for him.

Over the years research into the effects of unresolved grieving has determined that one or more of five different reactions are likely to surface. The first reaction, as shown in the above example, is addiction to alcohol, drugs or both. Other reactions include mental illness and acute depression. Those who suffer from these often attempt suicide and a good portion of them will be successful. A fourth reaction is abuse of food to the point where the person becomes grossly overweight. Neurotic behavior is the fifth common reaction.

As I think about the clients I have seen, most of them have shown at least one of these and some have had all five. Among Natives, the most common reaction is that of alcoholism. An estimated 80 percent of our people have a major drinking problem. They may not all be alcoholics but they at least are drinking to the point where it affects their lives and the lives of their families in a negative way.

The years 1958 through 1970 were the ugly years of my life. During this time my addiction problem, which had never been dealt with, re-asserted itself and I suffered relapse after relapse. I wanted desperately to live a good, stable Christian life but I just could not.

After I completed treatment for a fourth time I heard a lecture on addiction. It informed me of the great strength of my mortal enemy, alcoholism. Like Samson of the Bible who was betrayed by Delilah, we must grow our seven locks of hair again before we can rise up to defeat our enemies. This lecture also taught me about the power of addiction and why it has been such a barrier to developing strong, enduring Christian character. I knew this was not only my problem but also the problem of vast numbers of our Indian people. We want to serve the Lord but in spite of our best efforts to remain sober we find ourselves back to drinking again and again.

I learned that addiction is an uncontrollable, over-powering urge, drive or force that becomes stronger than all other drives. It becomes the most important thing and the most demanding thing in our lives. There doesn't seem to be anything more powerful than those addictive needs. Addiction becomes the one primary urge that demands satisfaction above all else.

It is hard for most people to understand this. Normally, the most powerful needs we have are hunger, sex, and survival or self-preservation. Addiction is stronger than all of these. It is more important, more urgent than hunger, even stronger than sexual drives. It overpowers the need to survive. Doctors told us what alcohol was doing to our physical systems but we went right back to drinking in a very short time. In spite of the warning many of our drinking buddies drank themselves to death.

The people around us who witness this behavior conclude we must be crazy, insane or absolutely devoid of any kind of moral strength. Certainly that is what it feels like and it leads many an alcoholic to suicide who does not realize that the root of the problem is a physical addiction. They have lost the meaning and purpose of life and feel there is nothing left to live for. I know. I have been there. If these people understood their addiction and the fact that we have a program that can effectively arrest it, how differently they might react to it all.

Addiction is very powerful and it is highly underestimated. The Apostle Paul wrote in the Bible,

> *For I want to do good but I do not. I do not do the good I want to do. Instead I'm always doing the sinful things I do not want to do (Romans 7:18,19).*

I know this is talking about sin in general but it also applies so well to chemical dependency. Addiction is the thing that causes us to do what we don't want to do and which renders us incapable of doing what we know is right. The urge to satisfy an addiction is incurable. It is a chronic state, much as leukemia and diabetes are. Once you have them, you have them for life. We talk of arresting these diseases, never healing or curing them. Once a person is addicted the experience of intoxication has been indelibly etched within the mind. It remains the most intensely personal experience one can undergo. As time passes, with sobriety or staying clean, the urge becomes less powerful and does not recur as often but it does return.

Having said all this about the power of addiction I must not leave you with the impression that there is no hope. There is.

Some find spiritual solutions. Others need both the spiritual and treatment approaches. Take my family for example. I am one of six children and we all had major problems with alcohol and drug dependency. Of these six, two invited Christ into their lives and were delivered from their alcoholism. Both are serving the Lord today. Another brother and I have needed the help of Alcoholics Anonymous to sober up. Once that happened we were able to re-commit our lives to Christ and are now living consistent, stable Christian lives. The last two also became Christians but since they did not deal with their addiction problems they suffered relapse after relapse. Both eventually died of acute alcoholism.

I accepted Christ in 1947 and graduated from Bible school without ever dealing with my alcohol addiction problem. The church, the Bible school, Christian friends and fellow ministers were not able to help though they tried diligently for more than thirteen years. I would repent, return to church for a while, and then relapse. I continued to do this over and over again in spite of my best efforts to change. I had to go through treatment for chemical addiction four times before I was able to understand the spiritual principles of the AA program and come to practice them. Certainly it is God who delivered me from my alcoholism but He used the AA program and the treatment centers to do it. I also know that if I were to take another drink, then 10,000 would not be enough.

The AA program consists of twelve steps based on some very sound spiritual principles. For example, Step Three says, "We made a decision to turn our will and our lives over to the care of God as we understand Him." In so doing we should be making a strong commitment of our wills to a new way of life, a way of life governed by spiritual guidelines.

In my own experience I needed to get in touch with the truth, embrace it, to live life by a new standard of rigorous honesty and integrity. I had to make restitution to those I had harmed or cheated. I had to learn to forgive. As an AA member I learned that humility must become a new characteristic of my life; that I must commit all my shortcomings and defects of character to God and ask Him to remove them.

Then according to Step Twelve, I was to become a "missionary" to other alcoholics. No one else was having any success in helping them to recover and maintain sobriety. By becoming involved in these principles I found myself able to stay sober at last.

Seventeen years have now passed since I took that last drink. I did not like AA at first. I tried every other avenue that offered hope. Then, as a last resort, I turned to AA and found the help I needed. Since then I have often wondered why I had waited so long.

I thank and praise God for the good sobriety I have attained and maintained. I thank Him, too, for the AA program that He used to bring about my lasting sobriety.

One thing I learned from my thirty-five years of drinking is that when a person hits bottom as an alcoholic he also hits bottom spiritually. He arrives at a place where he has no character strength, no moral strength and no spiritual strength left. This is a pathetic place for a person to be but it's where every alcoholic ends up.

I went through Bible school. I was trained for ministry and I even served as a missionary before I fell back into drinking. I am sure many a person who had worked with Indians thought that all old Art had to do was repent, return to the Lord and he would be right back up there where he was. It doesn't work that way. It needs to be understood that when a person hits rock bottom this means spiritually too.

Once I sobered up, my wife and I had to begin to rebuild our spiritual lives from scratch. There was no quick cure. It took thirteen years of growth before God finally saw that we had matured enough to be used again in ministering to others the way I had when I first got out of Bible school.

I am going to say something that will upset some people a great deal: I feel strongly that Christian leaders and church people need to hear it.

From reading my Bible and knowing what it teaches, I should think the best place for an alcoholic to live would be in the shadow of the church. It is here he should be learning to rebuild his life based on biblical principles. I firmly believe the church has the answer and all the spiritual power necessary to get people with addiction problems back on their feet. Every alcoholic should be able to come to the church today and get the help he needs. Unfortunately—and I know there are exceptions—most churches shun alcoholics. Unable to get the help they need from the most logical source, statistics tell us that 75 percent of alcoholics die in their alcoholism.

I remember a conversation with the Rev. Gordy Grimm, head chaplain at Hazeldon Treatment Center, Center City, Minnesota. He told me of a survey taken in 1973 among alcoholics who were in recovery. Sixty-seven percent of them said,

> *"We went to the church first. We went to the clergy in our desperation for help but we didn't get it. We had to turn to AA and there we found the help we needed."*

Also, 68 percent of the respondents who had major mental and emotional problems said that they too went to the church and the clergy for help with the same result:

> *"We couldn't find it. We had to turn to psychology and to psychiatry for that help."*

As a member of the clergy I blush with shame when I hear this kind of testimony against the church. This should not be. There is something missing, a gap that needs to be filled. From what I can see, treatment programs like Alcoholics Anonymous are almost the only alternative. The facts show that 67 percent of the alcoholics who are sober today have achieved sobriety through AA.

I found the strength of AA to be in the way it helped establish the individual in living by spiritual principles. (In my case one of the principles I very badly needed was honesty.) The church should have been doing that for me but it wasn't. I was never taught anything about living by spiritual principles like that. AA forced me to do it. They made it plain.

> *"If you don't start becoming honest with the group, with yourself and with God, then get back out on the street until you're ready or until the stuff kills you."*

Faced with that kind of alternative I had no choice. I had to think about some real turning around. I knew if I was going to make it I must start doing what this program was telling me to do.

Today, as I look at both the church and AA, I am forced to say that what the church has not been able or willing to do, AA has done. It was AA that finally got me functioning as a Christian should. For that reason I have a lot of respect for the program. It opened the door for me when everyone else said that there was no door.

The church is missing a tremendous opportunity by not making use of one of the various addiction programs and the variety of local secular treatment centers. At the same time the church must be careful not to abandon the people it has placed in the centers. Visitation is a must. Be there to show you care whenever visiting is allowed. Be there as the individual progresses from one step to the next. If you are concerned that he needs faith in more than a mere higher power, be there to point him to the God of the Bible revealed in the person of Jesus Christ. As the need for building on spiritual principles is taught, use your Bible to give him the biblical foundation he needs.

If the church has been largely ineffective in ministering to alcoholics, one reason may be the lack of appropriate training in Bible colleges and seminaries. I know many missionaries who have done their utmost to deal with the needs of their Native congregations. They have worked with prayer and zeal and devotion to God but without much to show for their efforts. Part of the problem was they lacked the knowledge they needed. The training we have today is not offering us much of anything that will help us deal with the specific problems that Indians face, especially in the areas of grieving and alcoholism.

Though I have spoken highly of the merits of AA, programs like this are not the full solution. From my experience of working with Indians in alcohol treatment centers, I have had a growing conviction that for most

Indian people alcoholism is a symptom. It indicates that another problem, usually that of pathological grief, is the cause or root of the addiction. To treat one without the other is to leave the job half done. The sober but chronic mourner is still not going to grow spiritually and eventually he will slip right back into drinking. If it is pathological grief that triggered the alcoholism in the first place, then we need to deal with the grief as well as the addiction before that person can return to wholeness.

Adapted from *The Grieving Indian* by Arthur H. and George McPeek, Winnipeg: Indian Life Books, 1988.

OUR MOST DEADLY ENEMY

I am more powerful than the combined armies
    of the world;

I have destroyed more men than all the wars of
    the nations;

I am more deadly than bullets and I have wrecked
    more homes than the mightiest guns;

I am the world's slyest thief: I steal millions of
    dollars each year;

I spare no one and I find my victims among
    the rich and poor alike, the young and the
    old, the strong and the weak; widows and
    orphans know me;

I loom up to such proportions that I cast my
    shadow over every field of labor;

I lurk in unseen places and do most of my
     work silently;
You are warned against me but you heed not;
I am relentless;
I am everywhere—in the home, on the street,
     in the factory, in the office and on the sea;
I bring sickness, degradation and death and yet
     few seek to destroy me;
I destroy and crush, I give nothing and take all;
I am your worst enemy. My name is *Mr. Alcohol.*

THE GREAT REMOVER

Alcohol is good at removing things. If you have stains on
your clothing, alcohol might remove them. It will also
remove the winter clothes, spring clothes and summer
clothes from man, his wife and children if used in large
enough quantity.

Alcohol has been known to remove furniture from
the home, rugs from the floor, lining from the stomach,
health from the liver, vision from the eyes and judgment
from the mind.

It will also remove reputations, good jobs, good
friends, happiness from children's hearts, sanity, freedom,
man's ability to adjust and live with his fellow man and
even life itself.

As a remover *alcohol has no equal.*

Arthur Holmes is an Ojibwe Indian from Wisconsin. For thirty-five years he was an alcoholic. Because of drinking he lost his family, his career as a minister, many jobs, everything he owned and almost his life.

In the early 1970s, his wife put him in a treatment center. He came out sober and has stayed that way ever since.

After training in addiction counseling, Art worked in several Indian alcohol treatment centers. Today, he is continuing to serve as a minister among his own people.

IL: *How great a problem is alcohol among Indian people today?*

Art Holmes: It is a major problem. It presently affects about 80 percent of Native people. They may not all be alcoholics but they are creating major problems in their homes and communities because of it.

IL: *Can you describe the problem a bit more?*

Art: Sure. About 70 percent of all the treatment services given by the Indian Health Service, either directly or through contract services, are alcohol related. About 80 percent of suicide and suicide attempts are alcohol related and that is five times the national figure. In about 90 percent of killings among Indians, either the killer or the victim or both were drunk when it happened. Almost 100 percent of crimes for which American Indians are put in prison were committed under the influence of alcohol and 75% of fatal accidents among Native people are alcohol related.[1]

IL: *What are some of the side effects of alcohol among Indian people?*

Art: There is much violence. Among Indian people accidents are the number one cause of death. Homicide is number seven. Suicide is number ten. You can see from this that Indians are dying sudden, unexpected, violent types of deaths. Because of this they need professional help with their grieving but there is none available. Indians are a grieving people and there is no one qualified to help them. This bottled-up pain that they don't know how to handle leads to drinking.

IL: *But everyone is upset by death. How are Indian people different?*

Art: We are not dying the kinds of deaths the rest of society is dying. The rest of society is dying anticipated deaths: death is coming and they can handle that. Only 20 percent of them die unexpectedly compared with 80 percent of Indian people. Eight out of ten of our people need help from professionals but we are not getting it. These problems are all developing out of alcoholism and drug dependency.

Indians use chemicals to relieve the hurt, the pain, the loss that they're suffering because they don't know how to handle it. And so they drink, and continue to

---

[1] Based on a U.S. Government report

drink, because it deadens the pain and the misery, the grief, the hate, the bitterness they feel.

IL: *How does this affect the family?*

Art: Not everyone who drinks is an alcoholic but many drink to the point that welfare is putting their children in foster homes and orphanages and this creates another difficult problem. There is a lot of anger, resentment and bitterness that develops over these separations. Kids have a real hatred toward their parents for abandoning them. There are so many kids who are born to unmarried parents who fit in this group.

When I was working at the treatment centers I had to deal with this kind of grief and hurt almost on a daily basis—separation from parents, attitudes of hatred and hostility toward the welfare services that broke up their homes. Many have hatred and resentment towards the white foster homes where a lot of them have suffered so much child abuse and sexual abuse. By the time we get them at the treatment centers they are emotionally starved. And not only this; broken homes mean they miss out on the building of their consciences. Usually this is taking place between the ages of eight and twelve. If their values have not been set by their parents or by the church, then when they reach thirteen the peer group gets them and sets their values. I think you know what those are. We have to re-do all this for them when they come through treatment.

IL: *This must have a bad effect on the average life span of Native people.*

Art: It sure does. A few years ago the average life span of Indian people was about 44 years. There is some evidence that things are improving but it is going to take maybe twenty years to show up in the statistics.

IL: *Drinking costs money. How does this affect Indian people economically?*

Art: Eighty percent of Indian people drink too much and they can't afford it. I make more money than many of them and I can't afford it so I don't know how they can drink and stay drunk for the better part of a week. It is a real economic problem and it stops them from maturing.

Indians are not maturing nor is anybody who is on chemicals. It affects them mentally, emotionally, and spiritually. The only way they are growing up is physically, likely getting fatter and more gray.

A problem drinker cannot be depended upon. They are not able to take on responsibility and handle it properly. They have mental problems and emotional problems and need professional help.

IL: *How is alcohol affecting Native people culturally?*

Art: At one time American Indians did not drink. Now that they have started, their ability to function culturally has dropped below the level necessary to keep the culture going. Alcohol just wipes out the culture.

What usually happens at this point is that the culture will begin to seek some kind of unifying strength to help people fight back, but Indians have not been able to rally from alcoholism. When we sober up one it seems there are about three more just getting hooked on alcohol.

IL: *What should Indian people do?*
Art: One thing they should do is support the Alcoholics Anonymous program or something similar: this can be their surviving strength. Then they would be able to rise above this threat that is killing them. Indians have done this with everything else except alcoholism. For some reason the heads of the tribes are not looking at AA.

IL: *Are these programs, yours and others like it, successful?*
Art: Yes. From reports of the AA groups, and from the social service people we talk to, there is some success. For instance, in one community they see a remarkable change. Fifteen years ago when we would walk through the town about three-quarters of the Indians were drunk or drinking. Now there are only a few. This is in Minnesota; other states are just beginning to think about treatment centers. Some aren't doing anything.

IL: *Do you think there is something in the physical make-up of a person that makes him more likely to have a problem with alcohol than the next person?*
Art: I think some people will have more trouble than others. Drug companies know that about 12 percent of the total population will not be able to take any kind of drug. Twelve percent can't take aspirin. Twelve percent can't take insulin. It is the same with alcohol—12 percent can't

handle it. This holds true for Indian people just like any other race.

IL: *Then how do you explain the high percentage of Indians who have problems with alcohol?*

Art: Indians are drinking for specific purposes, for emotional help. They are self-medicating themselves with these drugs and alcohol. They are using chemicals to deaden themselves to the pain they feel.

IL: *Are there programs you would recommend to help the alcoholic?*

Art: I heartily recommend AA and treatment centers. The steps of AA will lead a person back to taking responsibility for his own problems. They will lead the person into a spiritual experience if those steps are followed correctly. This is what made a Christian out of me. Up to that point I was only religious. I see it doing the same for others. AA opens the door to everyone.

IL: *Do God or the church have a part to play in helping to fight alcoholism?*

Art: I would say the church has the answer, or should have it; but since just about everything supernatural has been taken out it has just become another organization in many cases. When the church shuts the door on the Holy Spirit and His work then that church isn't able to help anyone.

IL: *What success rate do you see for Indian alcoholics who dry out?*

Art: At our center about one out of three stays sober. There is a difference between "sober" and "dry." A sober person is one who is in good recovery. He is able to take responsibility again and is enjoying life. A fellow who is dry is filled with all the same compulsion to drink and is just waiting for another chance to get at it.

IL: *Why do some centers have a poorer recovery rate than this?*

Art: They let people go too soon. The average person takes seventy-two hours to dry out but if that person has been drinking for many years this isn't enough time. In seventy-two hours he is just about ready for DTs (delirium tremens: tremors and hallucinations experienced by people who are drying out). At the time when he needs help the most they discharge him.

IL: *Can alcoholism be passed on from parents to children?*

Art: There is a general rule that what parents do in moderation, children will do in excess. This often holds true for alcohol abuse. Children are also affected in other ways. Babies born to drinking mothers have been born drunk, with liver problems, mental retardation and all sorts of physical deformities.

IL: *Has the age level of alcoholics among Indian people changed much in the last ten years?*

Art: They are much younger than they used to be, on the average about thirty. It starts with those as young as thirteen or younger and goes on up to the elderly.

IL: *What advice do you have for the Indian alcoholic?*

Art: My advice would be to seek out the alcohol counselor in his area and take the advice he gives. It is a lot easier to get Indians into treatment now than it was ten years ago. They can talk about it without getting mad. They are resigned to it and aren't fighting it like I fought it eighteen years ago. They should also get in touch with local treatment groups like AA or Alcoholics Victorious. Here they can get support from others who are going through the same struggles.

IL:: *What advice do you have for others?*

Art: Drugs and alcohol are here to stay. They are affecting our Indian people in the spiritual realm. We need to deal with that spiritual realm on the basis of God in Christ. Our people need to make a personal commitment to Jesus Christ first. This takes care of the sin problem. Then God's power is available to deal with the alcoholism. If we don't deal with drugs and alcohol they will deal with us.

Then there is grieving. Help Indian people deal with their grief and most of the reasons for drinking are taken away.

*From college athlete to junkie, his life was a
downward spiral until he thought he was...*

Beyond Hope
by Jim Sky

"Jim," my wife said as I walked in the door. "I want you to make a decision." Putting a quart of whiskey on the table, she gave me an order demanding that I make a choice.

"This bottle or our marriage!" she demanded.

"That's easy," I replied. I picked up the bottle. "I'll see you later!"

My two daughters came out of the bedroom. They were only four and five at the time.

"Daddy, please don't go!" they cried, "Daddy, don't go!"

I walked to the front door, picking them up.

"Honey, I love you very much, but I have to leave." That's all I said.

With that, I walked out the door never to see them again for seventeen years.

For some, this experience would have seen the end. But for me, it was just more of the same old thing. My life was a downer, almost from the start.

I was born the child of an unwed mother. Unwanted, I was left at birth in an orphanage in Chippewa Falls, Wisconsin. At age two, I was placed in a foster home in Ashland, Wisconsin. I lived with my foster parents until I was 17.

From an early age, I felt I didn't belong. I felt "different." After all, I was an unwanted child and therefore a misfit. I can remember one time when I was about four or five years old. I was feeling all alone. Running across a hay field crying, I tripped and fell. Just lying there on the ground, I felt a warm feeling come over me. I sensed then that it was love. Way back then I believe the hand of the Lord was on me, but I didn't understand it much until later.

By the time I started school, I was often beaten up by older kids. But as I grew older, it wasn't long before I was able to take care of myself. I learned how to fight, and fight I did. Fighting was my way of speaking my mind and releasing my feelings. Before long, others began respecting me for my fighting.

I was a good athlete. In high school I became a star in football, basketball and baseball. I also was an above average student. For many years, being good was what I did best. I got a lot of praise and acceptance for that. I think that I was doing those things to be accepted, because of the feelings of rejection working in me. But there was a time when I no longer got acceptance and praise for being good. It became the normal thing and was what was expected of me. I started hanging around with people who weren't so good. I started having bad attitudes and doing terrible things and getting accepted for that.

I began drinking when I was 15. Shortly after that, I was arrested and placed in jail for car theft. This was my first experience with the law. But it certainly wouldn't be the last.

At 17, I received a football scholarship to the University of California where I got my degrees in sociology and psychology. During my years at the university I got involved in the drug scene. I started using heroin and morphine. It wasn't long before I had a $250-$300 a day habit. I began transporting narcotics to pay for my drug addiction. It was a very well-paying job and I made a lot of money doing it.

During my college days, I met and married my wife and we had our two daughters. After six years, my wife made me choose between her and the bottle. I chose the bottle.

I kept right on delivering drugs. It wasn't long before I got busted. I ended up in prison for seven years. During those prison days I did some boxing and other recreational activities, but I never did anything to change what was down inside of me.

While I was in prison I completely lost my family. My wife divorced me and I had no idea where she or my daughters were.

When I was released, I went right back to doing what I did best—drinking alcohol and using drugs. This took me all over the country—Chicago, Los Angeles, Minneapolis and everywhere in between.

In Chicago, I walked into the Pacific Garden

Mission. There I heard the song "Softly and Tenderly, Jesus is Calling." With disgust, I got up and walked out.

The second time I heard this hymn was in Los Angeles. Just as I sat down the organist started playing that song. I got up and walked out. I just couldn't stand to hear that song.

My travels finally took me to St. Paul, Minnesota where my addictions continued in their downward spiral. My time in this city was perhaps the darkest period of my life. I was picked up 104 times by the St. Paul police for drunkenness. I was placed in fifteen different treatment centers trying to get rid of the addiction problem. While in St. Paul, they sent me to Detox over 100 times. Finally, they told me not to come back. They said there was no hope for me.

I lost everything—my material possessions, my self-respect and every meaningful relationship I ever had.

One night—December 14, 1982—while sleeping in a cardboard box, I had a dream. I saw my casket being carried out. I woke up terrified.

"God!" I said, "If you're real, I ask that you take my life. I don't want to live anymore. I've made a mess of my life. I've hurt a lot of people and I'm sorry for what I've done. If you're for real, I ask that you take my life."

After awhile, I got up from the snow and walked over to the Union Gospel Mission. A man was there talking about how Jesus died on the cross for our sins. He said that I no longer had to walk in the guilt of judgement over the things of past. He told us that we can have freedom and liberty from the bondages that bind us.

The man asked if anyone wanted to make a decision to let God take control of his life. My hand went up automatically. I remember looking at my hand and saying to myself, "Boy, you've flipped out now."

Then the man asked us to come forward. I got up and went forward. About half-way up the aisle, I got scared and turned around. There were two drunks sitting on the back row with me.

"If I go up front, so do you," I said.

I was big and mean. Usually when I spoke, people listened. The three of us went forward that night to give our lives to the Lord. We got saved that night.

God instantly delivered me from the desire to drink and do drugs. I stayed at the mission for a year in their program called *Christ Recovery Center.* It's a 12-step recovery program. That's where I started to get my life back together again.

I met another girl who had been walking with the Lord for seven years before she met me. She and I got married and started a street ministry in downtown St. Paul. Also, at the same time I was sharing God's Good News on various Indian reservations in the U.S.

Then I felt a call to go back to the St. Paul Union Gospel Mission.

I was praying faithfully that someday, somehow, the Lord would get me back together with my children. I started getting letters telling me where they were. One letter told me that I was already a grandpa. I heard that both my daughters were married and one of them had a son.

I drove back up to northern Wisconsin. I found out where they were living and went up to the house and knocked on the door. I'll never forget my feelings when my oldest daughter answered the door. She looked at me and just started crying. Falling into my arms, she cried tears of joy.

Then she took me up to her room.

"I've got to show you something." Underneath the bed was a cardboard box. She started showing me all the things I bought her when she was a little girl.

"I saved these things," she cried, "because I knew one day you'd be back."

The next day I met my other daughter. The same thing happened. God answered our prayers and brought us back together!

I didn't know if my foster mother was still alive. She was the one who prayed continually for me. I finally got up the nerve to call and see if she was still living. She was.

I drove up to see her. I hadn't seen her for many years. She met me at the door, tears streaming down her cheeks.

"My Jimmy's found the Lord!" she cried. She had been praying for me all those years, not knowing what had become of me, but believing God would answer.

My foster mother had thirteen foster children. I was the last one she raised. Spending several days with her, I was able to tell her how the Lord saved me.

A year later, I got a call telling me that she was very ill. Again I drove up to her place. She told me once again how very real the Lord was. "God really does answer prayer!" she said while on her deathbed. "All my dreams and prayers have been answered." Shortly after that she died.

In 1988, I was adopted by the Great Lakes Bad River Tribe in northern Wisconsin. This is the tribe I was born into.

I believe we go through life looking for an experience that will change who we are, what we think and what will bring us good. But the only one who can do this is Jesus Christ. Drugs, sex, music or any of that stuff just doesn't deliver. It's just vanity. I've done it all.

Phillippians 2:13 tells us that "God is working in you. God is helping you obey Him. God is doing what He wants done in you" (NLB). I believe it is God's hand on us that makes us willing. It's the experiences we go through that God uses to make us willing to do His will. Just like the prophet Jonah. He didn't want to go to Nineveh. But he had an experience that changed his life. Whether we go first class or "fish" class, the hand of the Lord is on us and His purpose will not be stopped.

I've gone through it all. I've come to the simple understanding that Jesus Christ meets all my needs and desires. He can be all you need if you give Him a chance.

The Trade
by Buffalo

As I, Buffalo, came walking up to our cabin I was happy in my heart. I would be able to tell Good Woman, my wife, that God had blessed us again. My traps had been full this morning. Because the spring in my legs was no more, I could not set the long traplines of my youth, but the Lord had blessed the few traps that I could put out.

My body was tired. The day had been hard and the load I was carrying was heavy. But inside, in my heart, I was not tired. I still felt young, alive, and full of strength.

I wanted to surprise Good Woman. Maybe I'll just take one fur in and say, "This is all we caught." Then I'll wait a while before I bring the rest in and watch her as she becomes all happy and excited.

While I thought about how I wanted to surprise my wife, all of a sudden I heard someone inside the cabin crying. I felt heaviness in my heart and a fear. "What could have happened?"

As I opened the door slowly and looked inside, our little girl was crying and Good Woman was holding her in her arms and crooning to her and comforting her. At once I forgot my plans for a surprise. Quickly I stepped inside with all my furs still on my back.

Good Woman looked at me. I could see anger and despair on her face. Before I would ask her what was wrong, the words came rushing out of her. "That good-for-nothing cousin of yours, he should be run out of the village!"

Fear spread through my whole body. "What has he done to Corn Blossom?" I asked.

"Nothing," Good Woman said, as she began to talk more slowly. "He has not hurt Corn Blossom."

"Then what is wrong?" I asked.

"Remember when the Lord blessed you that day and you came home with two deer? We were so thankful that we would have fresh meat to eat and some to dry for the winter. Remember how Corn Blossom said that your cousin Brave Heart's children were hungry and you gave them one of the deer you killed?"

"Yes," I said, impatiently. "That was only two days ago. But what has gone wrong?" Good Woman ignored me and continued with her story.

"Corn Blossom went over to play with Cunwintku. When she came home she did not look happy, so I asked her, 'Did you have a fight with your cousin?' Then she started to cry, and had a hard time telling me what had happened.

"She said to me, 'Remember when we gave the deer to uncle? I was happy because I knew they didn't have anything to eat. Today, we were playing and my cousin said she was hungry. So I asked her if they ate all the meat already. She said they did not eat any of it. Her father took it somewhere and was gone all night. When he came home, he was drunk and the meat was gone.'"

By this time, Corn Blossom was quiet. Good Woman wiped the tears from her face and said, "Corn

Blossom, I want you to go and bring your cousins here. They will eat with us."

Suddenly I realized I was still standing there with furs on my back. As I put them down, Good Woman finally recognized how the Lord had blessed our small trapline.

"The Lord has been good to us," she said. By that time I had forgotten my furs. I was so mad at my cousin that I wanted to go over and knock some sense into his head. But I knew that would do no good. "What could have happened to Brave Heart?" I wondered. "Once he was such a good man. Even today, when he is sober, he has such a good heart."

I knew he was a slave to firewater, but I could not believe he would take food from his children to buy drink.[1] In my concern for him, I started to pace the floor.

"What kind of people would allow him to do such a thing? Don't they know what it does to his family? And Brave Heart's woman, the terrible things she does. Once they had a happy home, but now, to get firewater, he steals and lies and his woman sells herself. And the children are hungry and cold."

My thoughts turned to God and I cried out in my heart, "Oh, God, can you do something for our people? Can you free my cousin from firewater?[2] Can you give him a new heart? I know you gave your Son, Jesus, to die so that people like Brave Heart could be set free from firewater.[3] And I know you love us so much that you don't want to force anyone to turn to you. You want us to come to you because we need you, because we want to be set free. You don't want us to be slaves to sin. You want to give us a new heart. You want to make us a new people.[4]

"Oh, Great Spirit, Father God! There are so many of our people like Brave Heart and his woman. They do not have the desire to be set free. I don't think they want to change! Father God, can you reach their hearts by your Holy Spirit? Can you give them understanding? The life they live has made them like animals that have a sickness that drives them crazy! I know. I have seen these animals. And I know they are crazy for a time and then they die.

"Oh, Father God, you have made us higher than the animals. They die and their life is over. You have given us a spirit within that never dies. And when our body dies, our spirit goes on and lives forever. I know the Bible teaches that we all have to stand before you one day and answer for the life we have lived. I know the only way we can escape punishment for wickedness and for our sin is by believing that Jesus paid for our sins.[5] I know that believing that Jesus paid for our sins is not enough. We have to receive Him and let Him live within us.[6] When He lives within us, He can set us free.

"Father God, will you speak to our people? Will you give them understanding so that they will know that even though you love them, if they do not receive Jesus, one day you will have to punish them? And this punishment will never end. And they will not be able to escape by making their minds empty by drinking firewater."

As I finished my prayer, Corn Blossom came rushing

into the cabin with Brave Heart's children. I could see joy in their faces already because they knew they were going to eat. My heart was happy.

As I watched the children, Father God seemed to say to me, "See, if Brave Heart and others would come to me, I could satisfy their hunger, too. I would fill their emptiness with peace and they would have no more need for firewater."[7]

I knew it was true and I looked forward to that day.

The numbers in the story go with the following verses from the Bible. It would be good if you looked them up to read them.

[1] Proverbs 20:1 [2] John 8:36 [3] Romans 6:2,3 [4] John 3:14-16
[5] Romans 6:23 [6] John 1:12 [7] John 6:35; Ephesians 5:18

An Indian Mother Shares
Her Heartache for a Troubled Son

I remember I was young and he was very young. I held his fragile hand tightly in mine as we stood on the sandy road together.

We had been picking blueberries when he remembered that "big hungry bears live in the forest." He had come to me with his fear.

"Mommy, what if a bear comes? What will we do?" His moist brown eyes were full of fear and uncertainty. The questions hung between us, pulling the corners of his small mouth downward. Watching me, he stood, waiting for a mother's wisdom to chase away the disquieting images that claimed his thoughts.

I pressed his thin fingers between mine as I considered my words. I stooped down to meet him at his own level.

"Son," I said slowly, "any bear that tried to hurt you would have to deal with me first. I would kill him before I would let him hurt you."

He stared at me. He heard the terrible fierceness and conviction of my voice. And he was comforted.

Many years passed and once again I stood with him, this time against the social "bears" of drugs, alcohol and pot. I held his hand, now larger than my own. I heard my weeping voice calling his name. "I'm here," I said. I wanted him to know. My mind stumbled at the edge of this awful reality that I could not share.

"Neither life nor death nor drunkenness nor overdose shall be able to separate you from my love," I told his unconscious body. "My son, my son, oh Absalom, my son" (just like King David grieved for his son in II Samuel 18:33). I held myself tightly together as I entered alone into the pit of human despair that yawned darkly before me.

Later I spoke with him through a narrow slot in a metal door. He would not meet my gaze. He mumbled and was ashamed.

The judge had his say, and I embraced my son, the tall young stranger who wanted no more of my protection. Then I sent him off to an institution, feeding a fragile hope that he would return whole and free and comforted.

Where Were You, Mommy?

My heart was in the bars instead of at home. I wanted my children to be safe so I always did my drinking away from home. My drinking friends did not even come around the house. And before I left I made sure my children had food. I thought this was all I needed to do to keep my family safe, but it wasn't.

As soon as I left, drunken relatives would come to help themselves to the food and use the home. They would bring their girlfriends and take over the bedrooms. If they felt like having a party they did it in my home and told my children I had given them permission: but they lied. When my children complained to me I ignored them. My heart was in the bars instead of at home.

Please see and read all the things I am saying. Perhaps you are forgetting your family like I was. I had some very selfish excuses that let me shrug off my responsibility. When we are not home we leave our children wide open to all kinds of danger—an older brother's male friends or a sister's friends and boyfriends. Young children cannot handle situations like this. When something goes wrong we blame the older kids but it is really our fault. We should have been there. Instead we shrug off our responsibilities as parents. We see it as a good way to ease our guilt for what happened.

Another thing is money. When my children would come to ask for money I would give it to them to get rid of them. I sort of paid them off so I could leave to go drinking. Or I would promise them something and then forget about it. How badly we treat our children because we are drunk or don't remember. We may provide food and clothing for them but they are starving for love and affection.

Please, mothers and fathers, wake up! Find out how beautiful your children are. Tell them you love them while they are still around. I did, and I'm so glad. I praise the Lord today for the beautiful family He has given me. I can now love my children the way I should because God put His love in my heart. I still have some children at home. The rest have grown and have their own families. I like to read the Bible to the ones who are still with me. And we talk about how wonderful Jesus is.

Since I asked Christ to be part of my life I can see more clearly how His love can change a parent's heart for the best. I know this for a fact because I was an alcoholic mother. But praise the Lord, He cured my alcoholism the day I committed my life to Him. I wish I had done this years earlier so my children would not have had the tough times they went through alone.

God changed me; I know He can change you, too. He can make you into the parent you ought to be and He can help you be there when your children really need you.

CHAPTER TWO

Do the Memories of Abuse
Still Haunt You?

THE CRIME THAT
WILL NOT GO AWAY
by Jim Uttley

This crime has reached epidemic proportions. Not crimes like breaking and entering, terrorism, or murder. The crime is happening as you read these words. This crime involves theft, desecration and violence. In most cases it also involves cover-up.

We're referring to *child sexual abuse*. These three words, put together, ought to be an oxymoron: they don't fit together. Instead, in reality, they are almost the same.

In recent years when referring to child abuse in the North American Aboriginal community, it is usually in connection with the residential school system. Started in the late 1800s in the United States and the 1920s in Canada, the governments had a plan to assimilate Aboriginal people into the dominant society. Part of the process was to take children away from their families and place them in church and mission schools. Tragically, many of the caregivers abused their power by verbally, physically and sexually abusing those under their care. Thousands have come forward to tell their stories and seek compensation for the pain and trauma they endured as children and teenagers in these schools.

It is time to change our thinking about child abuse: it didn't happen only in residential schools and it didn't stop when the schools were closed. There is this thinking that if we just deal with the residential school issue we will bring healing and closure to this terrible chapter in history and in some way do away with child abuse in the Aboriginal community.

Yes, we do need to see justice demonstrated and survivors receive some sort of compensation but, more importantly, we need to realize child sexual abuse is continuing today and what went on in those schools pales in comparison to what's happening today. The children and grandchildren of survivors of residential schools are suffering the same pain and brokenness of their parents to an even greater degree. They are also continuing the vicious cycle of abuse.

The percentage of abuse survivors who become abusers is staggering. Does this mean that the majority of victims become abusers? No. Even if they don't turn around and sexually abuse others they often cope with their pain through anger, anxiety and fear. Their families pay a painful price.

For people who have not been abused it may be difficult to comprehend what happens to someone who is abused. As Kim Stewart has so aptly written in her article, *Sexual Abuse: Where is the Hope?* "The invisible damage done by sexual abuse hurts the mind, will and emotions. Bruises heal, but the imprint on the mind of all these types of abuse stays."

As much as one desires to push it back into the subconscious mind, the imprint is still there. When children are sexually abused it is much more than assaulting their bodies. It is giving them something they are not prepared to have while, at the same time, stealing from them what they cannot do without—their very childhood. It forces them to become adults overnight.

Even though all survivors become adults in body, many have their emotions and spirits locked in time and space at the point when their abuse occurred. There are three kinds of survivors of child sexual abuse:

1) Survivors who, in order to cope, have managed to push their experiences into the far reaches of their minds and souls. Without intense probing they may not even be able to remember any abuse. Outwardly they appear fairly normal, although they may have some addiction or compulsion such as drinking, smoking, or an angry temper. To the untrained eye or ear they are normal.

2) Survivors who have constant reminders of their abuse and yet deal with it in secret. They also may appear to have relatively normal lives.

3) Survivors who have neither been able to forget nor

deal with their abuse and therefore can't get past that point in their lives. Many have turned to alcohol and drugs. Their lives are quite unstable. Their family relationships and marriage situations are often disastrous. Many times their abusive past has led them to become perpetrators of abuse.

If you are a survivor of childhood abuse, which type are you? Perhaps you are a combination of these or you may not fit into any of these categories.

As a survivor I would probably fit mostly in the second category, but there's a part of me that would fit in number three. For over thirty years hardly a day would go by that there would not be some memory of that terrible time in my life when someone violated me. Because this was not a subject that people talked about I never knew that what I endured had the name "sexual abuse."

Once I could put a name to it, I was able to deal with it. I was able to discuss it with others, receive advice, counsel and encouragement to forgive my abuser, which I did. Not only that, but had a frank discussion with him. While I didn't feel he repented of his wrongdoing, the mere fact that I confronted him and was able to forgive, released me and set me free.

Dr. Dan Allender, counselor of sexual abuse survivors and author of *When Trust is Lost*, says that

> *Forgiveness means you are willing to let go of what someone owes you for the hurt he caused. God has shown you a far greater kindness. Yes, the offender*

and the silent parent(s) and likely many others owe you a lot. They could not repay what they owe you in a thousand lifetimes. But what we owe to God is even greater. It has no limit.

Please don't get the idea that this is easy. It will be one of the most painful things you will have to do—almost as painful as the abuse itself, but if you want full and complete healing, then you must forgive whether or not you are able to confront your abuser. All the monetary compensation in the world will not bring true freedom from a horrendous past. Only learning to forgive and let go will set you free.

What is Sexual Abuse?

It is important to understand what sexual abuse really is. In order for us to receive healing we must understand the original abuse. We must also understand the continuing damage that such abuse does to both offenders and victims.

Sexual abuse happens when a defenseless person (usually a child or a teenager) is used for the sexual excitement or pleasure of someone older, stronger or with more authority.

Sexual abuse includes much more than forced, unforced or make-believe sex. It includes any touching, rubbing, or patting that is meant to bring sexual pleasure to the offender. It may also include things the offender shows or says or makes the victim think about. Sometimes there is no touching at all.

- *Visual sexual abuse* ("visual"- what you see) may involve showing a victim pornography (books, magazines or videos) or any other sexually tempting scene. (For example, someone having a shower, people having sex, or people with some of their clothes off.)

- *Verbal sexual abuse* is abuse with words. The words may be directly about sex or they may simply cause a child to think about sex. Verbal sexual abuse may involve trying to make a child do something wrong for the offender's pleasure or trying to make the child feel dirty and ashamed.

- *Psychological sexual abuse* is abuse of the thoughts or feelings of the victim. One way it can happen is when the offender treats the child like a husband or wife, or like an adult friend or counselor. For example, a mother might tell her 12-year-old son about her sexual problems with his father. As she shares her deep thoughts and feelings with him she is causing him to have sexual thoughts and feelings that are too heavy and too adult for him. It just isn't right for an adult to make a child think about those kinds of things. It is harmful and confusing to the child.

Sexual abuse is a problem all over the world. Research suggests that in America alone, by the age of 18, one out of every three women will be a victim of sexual abuse involving touching. If we include sexual abuse that doesn't involve touching, the numbers are even worse. For instance, if we include victims of exhibitionism (when a person shows off his/her private parts) one out of two women are affected. When a man does this kind of thing to a woman she secretly wonders, "Why did he choose me?"

The numbers for men are not as well known. Men find it more difficult than women to admit they have been abused. Male victims and female victims are both haunted for a long time by upsetting questions about their own sexuality. The questions are there even though the victims have done nothing wrong. At one time it was thought that only two out of 100 men were sexually abused. New evidence shows that perhaps as many as one out of five have been abused.

We are now hearing of some family histories that include shameful things. In many cases abusers were themselves abused by parents or grandparents. Abuse passes silently from one generation to another as long as it is kept a "family secret." High expectations in society and in religious groups made people afraid to admit their problems.

These patterns of abuse have been made even stronger by recent problems: families breaking up, the spread of pornography, too much alcohol and drugs. Many people no longer have the courage to do the things they know are right and to speak out against those things that are wrong. Becoming involved in Satanism or other secret groups has also led some people to do sexual abuse.

God wants people to talk openly about sexual abuse. It's part of the written history of Israel. Read 2 Samuel 13:1-20. It is the story of King David's son Amnon who raped his half-sister Tamar and of all the trouble that followed. There is much to be seen in this sad event: a brother who did not control his own sexual desires; a sister not strong enough to defend herself; a father who did not try to make things right.

After being raped Tamar felt very badly and ashamed. Amnon hated Tamar. The family broke apart and there was more violence.

Some would say that all the trouble after the rape wouldn't have happened if Tamar had just kept quiet about it. That is not true! Tamar chose to show her sadness because her brother had wronged her and because he would not admit his sin. If Tamar had stayed quiet her brother's bad actions would have continued. He would have done to others what he did to her.

Because Amnon would not admit his wrong and ask for forgiveness and a chance to make things right, family anger grew. Two years later another of Tamar's brothers wanted revenge. Absalom killed Amnon, throwing David's kingdom into disorder. One life-shaking quake of sexual abuse sent tidal waves into the soul of Tamar and into many other lives.

The fact that God has included this event in His Word helps us to see how important it is for us to open our eyes to the terrible damage of sexual abuse.

Victims of sexual abuse often wonder how things that happened long ago can cause damage here in the present. The damage of the past is not erased by time.

Let's take an example. Let's say someone breaks an arm in an accident. The two parts of the broken bone may connect back together without the help of a doctor but they will probably be crooked. If a doctor helps right from the beginning the arm can become strong and straight. God wants the arm to heal well.

The damage caused by sexual abuse is a little like that broken arm. Time may take away some of the pain of the memories but it takes more than time to make the wound heal properly.

In the same way the damage caused by sexual abuse does not disappear when a person becomes a Christian. Following Christ is like fixing up a wonderful old house that badly needs repairs. The last owner destroyed its beauty but the new owner plans to make it as lovely as when it was first built. Every room must be redone. The fact that our lives are finally given back to God does not mean that every room is suddenly fixed up like new. People often refuse to allow God to work on certain rooms. We may not even know about a secret room on the top floor that is in bad shape.

Very often something keeps victims of sexual abuse from getting all of the repairs they need. Some people who were abused in the past say that the past cannot affect their life today. Other people do not even remember how badly they were hurt. Still others just say, "God is my new owner. I'm OK now." All of these people need to see clearly how they have been damaged. Only then can the repairs begin.

WHO IS AT RISK & HOW TO
IDENTIFY AN OFFENDER

Both girls and boys can be victims of sexual abuse. Girls are at higher risk. Offenders often target children who are isolated, who have little contact with friends, a sibling or an adult they can trust. Children with physical or mental disabilities are also more vulnerable to sexual abuse.

Children who have been sexually abused often exhibit certain signs. Being aware of them will alert you to the possibility that a problem exists. Keep in mind that a child may display some of these signs but be troubled about an entirely different matter. What must be considered in identifying the sexually abused child are:

1) Changes in behavior
2) Extremes in behavior from what is generally considered normal
3) The pervasiveness of a cluster of signs rather than a single indicator
4) The presence of these signs over a period of time, rather than a single occurrence

Some of the signs that a child has been sexually abused include:

- A change in appetite
- Becoming withdrawn
- Fear of a specific person or particular place
- Age-inappropriate behavior

- Phobias (fears of different things)
- Self-mutilation
- Poor academic performance
- Running away
- Aggressive behavior
- Delinquent behavior
- Physical ailments (headaches, stomach aches, etc.)
- Sleep disturbances (nightmares, bedwetting, etc.)
- Promiscuity (sleeping with many sexual partners)
- Venereal disease

How can I identify an offender?

The answer is simple: you can't. Contrary to the stereotype that deranged-looking strangers lurk in parks, abusers are normal looking individuals who can blend into any given neighborhood easily. Offenders come from all backgrounds without respect to age, race, religion, ethnic group, education or economic status. They can be either male or female although, in most cases, an offender is male.

Victims often continue to feel the effects of abuse long after it has ended, frequently into adulthood. Some block out the traumatic experience and may only realize the reasons for their difficulties later in life.

As a result of sexual abuse, victims may:

- Suffer from low self-esteem
- Carry around feelings of guilt, shame, and anger
- Feel isolated
- Abuse alcohol and drugs

- Turn to prostitution
- Suffer from eating disorders
- Have difficulty dealing with authority figures
- Have difficulty trusting
- Have difficulty forming healthy relationships
- Continue to experience feelings of victimization
- Attempt suicide
- Suffer from depression

Many victims successfully overcome the effects of their childhood sexual abuse. Once they start regaining a sense of control over their lives they are able to stop thinking of themselves as victims and begin thinking of themselves as survivors.

When sexual abuse is disclosed, you need to communicate the following messages to the child:

- "I believe you."
- "It's not your fault."
- "It should never have happened to you and I'm sorry that it did."
- "You were right to tell."
- "I care about you and will help you."
  You will also want to keep the following in mind:

- The child needs to be in a private setting and feel safe. Allow the child to set the pace. Avoid "interviewing" the child to get all the details.

- Your reaction can make a difference. A child who senses you are uncomfortable about learning of the abuse or the explicit language being used to describe the abuse may withdraw the allegation or be reluctant to continue talking. If you are unable to hold back feelings of anger about the abuse, let the child know that you are angry at what the offender did, not at the child.

- Validate the child's feelings. The child may be experiencing a range of emotions from fear and anxiety to anger and confusion, all of which are understandable under the circumstances.

- Don't promise the child you will keep the abuse a secret. The laws in your area may require you to report suspected child abuse. Other than informing the proper authorities you need to respect the child's right to privacy and avoid betraying the trust the child showed by disclosing the abuse to you.

- It is not your responsibility to determine if the abuse actually took place or to confront the alleged abuser. Your responsibility is to get assistance for the child. Contact the local child protection agency or other social service organization or the police.

FACTS AND FICTION ABOUT CHILD ABUSE

Myths about child sexual abuse exist as a result of misinformation and generalizations. The myths that are found within a given community depend on its experience with, and understanding of, child sexual abuse. Some of the more common myths are addressed here:

Myth: *Children lie about being sexually abused.*
Fact: Children rarely lie about being abused. Some may take back an allegation of abuse because they are afraid of the offender or, in cases of incest, to protect the abuser and maintain harmony in the family. This does not necessarily mean the abuse did not take place.

Myth: *Offenders abuse because they can't control their sexual needs.*
Fact: Although it may appear that offenders abuse to satisfy their sexual needs, child sexual abuse is really about control and power. This is why abusers target children who are vulnerable by the mere fact that they are dependent on adults for their physical, emotional, and economic needs.

Myth: *It isn't abuse if the child consents to the sexual contact.*
Fact: A child is not mature enough to realize the consequences of sexual contact with an adult and therefore can never be in a position to give informed consent. The

power difference that exists between a child and an adult makes any sexual contact abusive whether or not the child is perceived as having given consent.

Myth: *In most cases, the offender is a stranger to the child.*
Fact: In the vast majority of cases the victim knows and has an on-going relationship with the abuser. Offenders go out of their way to befriend children. They often seek out positions where they will have easy access to children, have authority over them and be able to gain their trust.

Myth: *Some children are seductive and provoke the offender into the sexual abuse.*
Fact: This is an attempt to place the blame on the victim. Abusers alone are responsible for controlling their actions and should not be allowed to rationalize their behavior.

Myth: *Offenders were themselves sexually abused and therefore aren't responsible for their behavior.*
Fact: While it's true that many offenders were sexually abused as children, this does not justify, excuse, or explain their actions. Not all victims of childhood sexual abuse go on to become offenders just as not all offenders were sexually abused.

Good Kids Make Good Victims

"We (unknowingly) train our children to be victims," claims Lt. Dick Willey, commander of the Child Abuse Unit for the Los Angeles County Sheriff's Department. Willey says that parents who try hard to be responsible and raise well-behaved children can actually set them up for abuse. Here are five key ways in which the value system of "good" kids can make them ideal victims:

1. Respect your elders. If an adult tells you to do something, do it!

Respecting authority is an area which Christian parents can easily oversimplify. Do your children know about misuse of authority? Has your family ever discussed proper times for disobedience?

2. Don't be a tattletale!

Willey stresses that the best way to protect...is to establish the rules early. "If anybody touches you and makes you uncomfortable, tell me. I don't care who it is—Daddy, Uncle, Grandpa, a neighbor—you tell me. We will make sure it doesn't happen again."

3. Children should be seen and not heard.

Many parents think they take time to listen but they don't take their children's thoughts or conversation seriously. A child who says Uncle Walter makes him feel "creepy" sometimes gets a rebuke but Dr. Meier, who heads Childhelp USA's research department, says those kinds of comments from a child should be listened to and followed up. "You should encourage, affirm and reward a child when he tells you his feelings," he says.

4. *Nice people don't talk about things like that!*

Children who never talk about sexual feelings with their parents have a very difficult time telling Dad or Mom if they are being molested. Parents should initiate and encourage positive, natural conversations about the role sexuality plays in God's plan.

5. *You're too big to cuddle!*

As children's bodies begin to mature, parents often withdraw physically. Many older children see this as a sign of rejection. Molesters look for withdrawn children who feel rejected and offer them acceptance in order to take advantage of them. One small victim explained, "Bad love is better than no love at all."

How to Raise a Sex Offender

"No way!" you say. "I'm going to raise my son right!"

That's what most parents say. Still, too many sons grow up to become sex offenders. In his paper on "New Myths About Child Abuse," David Finkelhor suggests several reasons why.

1. Tender Feelings are Sexualized

Little boys need to be cuddled and nurtured in ways that are not sexual. They need this from their father as well as from their mother. If they don't get this intimacy in childhood they will find it with their friends in adolescence. As adolescents, the intimacy they find will almost always turn sexual. The young man's mind forms a connection between emotional intimacy and sex. The only way he can think of to express his tender emotions is through sex. This man may marry and have a child of his own. As he cuddles and plays with his child, sexual feelings come up. Realizing that this is not appropriate the man may withdraw from his child and limit his physical contact. This starts the cycle all over again. Or, he may give in to his feelings and treat the child as a sexual object. Then the child learns to connect intimacy and sexuality even before adolescence.

2. The Attraction Scale

Many cultures train women to find their appropriate sexual partners among persons who are older, larger and more powerful than themselves. Men are encouraged to select their sexual partners from persons who are younger, smaller and weaker than themselves. This makes children attractive to men but not women. The man's mind forms a connection between power or authority and sex. As a result, some male doctors, therapists, pastors and employers become sexually involved with their patients, clients and employees. Children, the youngest, smallest and weakest, become the easiest targets for sexual abuse from men.

3. "Child Care—It's Not a Man's Job!"

Many men grow up not believing that an important part of their role is to care for and nurture children. "That's a mother's job," they say. If they do not get involved with children it is hard for them to identify with a child's point of view. In addition, they lose touch with their "inner child." They have no idea how children feel when relationships are sexualized or when they are betrayed by an adult.

To these reasons we would add…

4. Shifting of Boundaries (Proverbs 22:28)

Recently the Supreme Court of British Columbia struck down the section of the Criminal Code, which makes it a crime to possess child pornography. Our governments, schools and media seem uncertain about what is right and what is wrong. No wonder so many men and boys are making bad moral choices!

In raising sons, Finkelhor recommends:

(1) Take great care to allow space for tender feelings.
(2) Encourage boys and men to choose their sexual part-

ners from people of equal social status, intelligence and power.

(3) Encourage men to identify more with the needs of children.

And we add:

(4) Restore biblical boundaries for behavior.

These will be difficult to achieve in a society so filled with abuse. If you are a man or teenage boy, for example, it is very hard to get a job as a babysitter or daycare worker. Certainly we need the safeguards that are in place for these areas of child care but if we don't find ways to train boys and men to take healthy masculine responsibility for women and children, if we don't restore moral boundaries that protect everyone, the abuse is likely to continue.

Survivors of Abuse

by Phil E. Quinn

Shortly after the last beating his adoptive parents inflicted upon him, Peter was told to leave home and never return. He was seventeen. Something about him had changed during those years of violence. He was now tall, his young adolescent body strong and quick.

But it was not his stature that frightened his parents that night; it was his attitude. He did not cower and submit helplessly but stood tall and erect, his eyes burning a hole in the wall as blow after blow pounded the all too familiar pain into his body. Those eyes could no longer hide the seething rage and burning hatred. His parents saw that deadly intent, recognized it for what it was, and did what they had to do to protect themselves. They threw him out.

Once on the street, with no money and the knowledge that there would be no turning back, Peter sought ways to survive. After two weeks of living on scraps scavenged out of garbage cans and unable to find work, he was rescued by Satan's Saints, a group of bikers. Although Peter accepted their help at first, he had no intention of joining their ranks. He was not even sure they would want him.

Instead, he tried to join the military. He wanted a gun in his hands for only one insane reason—to kill people. He wanted to make other people hurt as he had hurt. By the age of seventeen Peter had been beaten into a homicidal rage.

The armed forces, however, would not take him; he was blind in his left eye. Rejected by his family, by society, and now by the military, Peter had little choice. He joined the bikers and, after the initial doubts and uncertainty, plunged headlong into molding himself into one of them. His thoughts, feelings, and appearance all changed so he could fit in. More than anything else he wanted to belong to someone, something, somewhere.

Like most victims of severe childhood trauma, Peter's personality had become distorted. What he had learned as a child he continued to believe as an adolescent and as a young adult: the world around him was a hostile place to which he did not belong; other people were untrustworthy and rejecting; he himself was totally inadequate, unworthy of love and acceptance. So his life continued with but one primary purpose—to survive.

Survivors of severe child abuse tend to have a strong resentment toward authority, any authority, but particularly that which they perceive to be unjust and directed toward them. Children learn to respect authority through their relationship with their parents. If all is as it should be, children learn to trust their parents for protection and for providing their needs. If those needs are not met, children quickly learn that in order to survive they must take care of themselves. Since they cannot trust their parents to take care of them they cannot afford to respect parental authority; to do so would threaten their survival. This attitude of self-sufficiency and distrust of authority usually will be carried into their adult lives. Trust and respect die at the hands of betrayal. Abused children are betrayed children.

As adults, people like Peter tend to still perceive themselves as victims. They continue to feel helpless in the face of life's demands. Unable to live up to the expectations of their parents, they have developed a life script of failure. As victims they do not have power either to control or to change their lives. In order to survive they cannot afford to assume responsibility for their own lives. To do so would be to court failure.

Unable to win parental approval they become convinced they cannot win social approval. They learned as children that to win approval involves living up to another person's expectations. Yet to attempt to do so only invites disappointment and failure and they cannot take the risk of more rejection. So most do not try. Believing they cannot earn approval they tend to seek attention through disapproval.

Most survivors of severe child abuse suffer from an inner emptiness. They are lonely, desperate people who cannot form close relationships. In order to have an intimate relationship with another person there must be trust, yet in order to survive they must trust no one. Many evolve into sociopaths who perceive other people as enemies and threats to their survival.

At the same time they are dominated by a deep sense of guilt. They blame themselves for their childhood abuse. If they had not been so bad, they believe, their parents would not have needed to beat them. They feel a need for punishment. Arrogance and defiance often shroud their sense of personal guilt—or for having been a child.

Raised in the midst of domestic and personal chaos many of these people also have a desperate need for structure in their lives. They need someone to take care of them. Some are most comfortable and feel most "at home" in prison.

On top of everything else, they tend to be deeply emotional. Their emotions are not glowing embers but raging fires. They often express themselves in violence. Perhaps this is why over 90 percent of the 1,500 individuals on death rows in the U.S., and over 80 percent of those who commit violent crimes, were severely abused as children.

Most of these people feel they have nothing to lose. They lost it all a long time ago. So they tend to maintain a high-risk posture toward life and other people. There is no one more dangerous than someone who has nothing to lose.

Perhaps most tragic of all, adult victims of severe child abuse tend to see life as "luck." They are constantly in search of the pot of gold at the end of the rainbow. Unable to take control of their lives and successfully direct them toward goals and achievements, they rely on chance for all rewards. The result is that they tend to seek gratification wherever they may happen to find it, regardless of the consequences.

Peter was no exception. He was a survivor. It did not take him long to become totally submerged in the biker life-style. He became one of them in every respect except

one: a faint, intangible flicker of hope! A hope that perhaps someday he would find someone who would love
him, accept him, believe in him, and—even more important—someone he could trust and love in return. It was
a dim hope that someday he could prove to himself and
to the world that he was not all bad, that he could be a
good and responsible person, deserving of respect. It was
a faint hope, but a hope that just would not die.

SEXUAL ABUSE: REASON FOR HOPE

by Kim Stewart

If you are a survivor of child abuse or know someone who is, don't be surprised if you feel overwhelmed with the enormity of it. Take comfort. There is hope and I encourage you to ask for help for yourself or your friend!

If you do not take care of your anxiety, fear, shame, guilt or anger you will become very tired. You may be depressed due to having made poor choices birthed out of the pain of your past. This situation leads to deeper depression, which can lead to thoughts of suicide. Perhaps you are tempted with thoughts of taking your life or know someone who is. Here are things you need to know and steps to take.

Those most at risk are people with a previous suicide attempt, people with mental disorders and/or who are on drugs and alcohol. Males are at greater risk than females.

When will a person actually try to take their life? Surprisingly, a person deep in depression may not be able to summon enough energy to commit suicide.

Once the decision has been made they may seem happier than they have recently been; they know their pain will soon end.

Review their recent past to see if there have been any potential "last straws" such as loss, additional stresses, lack of support or a hopeless type of pain. It may help you to know that people who are contemplating suicide often communicate their plans to others. If you observe someone collecting harmful objects, giving away valued possessions and becoming more withdrawn, take note. Making wills, a loss of enjoyment in activities previously enjoyed, self-blame and shame is also noteworthy. Prolonged agitation and/or insomnia, non-compliance with medication or treatments, lack of attention to physical care and expressions of hopelessness, verbalizing a desire to die are all a form of communication that this person could be at increased risk.

Don't be afraid to ask questions

Even with all the information I am not saying you are responsible for someone who commits suicide; I am saying you are responsible to try to prevent someone from doing it.

Do not be afraid to ask questions like, "Do you ever feel that you cannot go on? Do you ever feel that life is not worth living? Do you ever have thoughts of harming or killing yourself, even by 'accident'? Do you struggle with these thoughts often?" Asking such questions shows that you care, that you are listening.

If you get a positive answer to any of the above, do not demean or diminish the seriousness of what they are saying. Do not appear shocked. Ask if they have any plans and do not debate whether the plans are morally right or wrong. They are in the kind of pain that does not need more judgement. You need to show you care and you love them.

Talk about the pain the person is experiencing. You cannot solve all their problems: they need God. You can start them on a path to expose the lies they believe. Lies believed in childhood are hard to shake. If a child believes he or she is stupid or worthless because of shaming or abuse, it will take a greater belief in God's Word to know that they are valued and loved. If an adult believes that there is no purpose for their life, they need to know that God has plans for them—plans for a future and hope.

They will need a relationship with a loving and perfect God, one whom they can believe will tell them truth. As they think about the new truths they read in the Bible they will notice that the deception learned from the past weakens under truth.

So when you encounter someone sad or hopeless, be prepared to give an account for your hope..."This is my reason for hope. God does redeem!"

I am no stranger to suicide. Many years ago I lost a friend to suicide and became suicidal myself. Someone came along, just in time, and helped me. I do not know why no one came for my friend. Perhaps someone did and my friend chose another way. I do know that if I can share my hope in God, perhaps the saving of my life will bring more fruit by encouraging you to help save someone else's life. You can be the person who will be there just in time.

Live one day at a time

If you are the one who is contemplating suicide, I understand your pain. Put your trust in God and live one day at a time. I did not crawl out of my despair overnight. It took time. To this day I am more grateful for the healing and hope that has come out of my hopelessness than I am to have a roof over my head. God has walked me through this very worthwhile journey.

"May the God of hope fill you with all joy and peace as you trust in Him, so that you may overflow with hope by the power of the Holy Spirit" (Romans 15:13).

I work in a nursing capacity with a program that deals with adult survivors of childhood sexual abuse. The words "childhood" and "sexual abuse" do not belong together. Put together they describe an atrocity that should not be. I shudder to think what God must think of this.

This may be difficult, but let's look at an example of what may have happened to you or to someone you know.

A friend discloses to you a story from her past and she tells you how she prays for intervention for the bad situation she is in right now. She fights back tears and tells you that as far back as she can remember she has felt lonely, rejected and abandoned due to neglect stemming from parental alcoholism. Then, as she hangs her head in shame, she tells you there is more. Breaking your heart, she says she feels evil and dirty, confessing that as a child desperate for love and affection, she "allowed" herself to be sexually abused, first by her father, and then an uncle.

Questioning her, you might ask, "Have you ever told anyone about this?" And the all-too-common answer comes as she explains simply that if her present were not such a mess, she would leave her past in the past where everyone had told her it belonged. Then she offers a little more explanation and tells you she did disclose the abuse to her mother but was not believed. Moreover, her mother, out of fear, blamed, minimized, and then physically and verbally assaulted her.

There comes a shaky sigh and she reveals how, by withdrawing, she avoids the pain of rejection and comforts herself with drugs and alcohol. Depressed, she whispers how she struggles now to get out of bed, care for her children, and even food has lost its appeal. She slowly reveals that she has thought of taking her own life.

Hopelessness is a sign

Hopelessness is a sign. To those who never feel loved or comforted, and to those who feel helpless, suicide is sometimes seen as a welcome action.

The more abuse you have suffered, and the closer the relationship to the abuser, the more damaging the effect. The "invisible" damage done by sexual abuse hurts the mind, will and emotions. Bruises heal, but the imprint on the mind of all these types of abuse, stays.

Abusers think they can keep the sexual abuse "invisible" by trying to keep the victim quiet with bribes and a variety of threats. This, of course, speaks of their own guilt. Sometimes they will even force compliance and silence with threats to beat or kill other family members. They will often blame the victim for provoking the abuse in an attempt to transfer the responsibility of their own shame and deviant behavior on the child.

Reading this may compel you to great anger and yet the response of family members in which this has occurred can be rather surprising. They have been known to join the abuser in blaming the victim.

Often family members, each having their own agenda and fears, will sometimes minimize and discredit the accusations of the victim, even if they have seen the abuse. This, of course, leaves the victim unprotected and feeling more helpless.

Trust has become mistrust; love turns into a feeling of being unlovable; hope is crushed in humiliation and shame is ingrained. Dreams are now nightmares, self-esteem now self-hatred, a body used as an instrument of another's sin. In addition, the child is sometimes blamed or instructed by the abuser to take responsibility for the repeated assaults. The child turns the confusion and anger on himself or herself and generally feels that it is easier not to exist or feel. This causes a battle to rage that the child cannot win because inevitably feelings will, and do, arise.

You will need to lean on God

I would advise that before you embark on a healing journey, that you prayerfully consider a network of support and safety. And search yourself, asking God if now is the time for you. If it is, enlist good friends, a pastor, a support group or whomever God places on your heart as an instrument He can use to see you through. However, do not expect them to rescue you. You will need to learn to stand and rely on God. This means taking personal responsibility for your own journey and casting your cares on God. Pattern yourself after Jesus as an excellent example. He tells us to do so.

You may also need to put some distance, and set up some boundaries, physical and emotional, between you and the negative influences, such as drugs and abusive family members.

It will take faith-fed courage to defend those boundaries, especially those around your recovery. But know this, God is okay with boundaries—He set them up Himself in the Promised Land. Since the enemy wants what you have, including this potential for recovery, you must listen to the Spirit of God when someone has disturbed your peace. When peace is gone you know that you must be on spiritual alert and set up some extra spiritual guard when someone is threatening your recovery. We do not fight against flesh and blood, but against the powers of darkness (Ephesians 6:12).

It will help if you try to maintain a normalized life as much as possible during the process. Eat, sleep, relax and exercise, taking care of your body because, believe me, your mind will be working overtime during this process. Stay in the Word of God. You are not just in a healing process; you are in relationship-building time between you and God, then between you and others.

As you walk this recovery out you will need to use many tools. Emotions are one of them. They are neither good nor bad and they are not who you are! They are just information that lets you know what is going on inside. Listen to them! Change your thinking and understand that you do not have to feel good all the time to be emotionally healthy.

Your emotion at times may be uncomfortable and the enemy will whisper, "Medicate it!" The devil does not want healing. But hooray and hallelujah!...God gave emotions to all of us to help us in our growth. You cannot grow spiritually if you do not listen to them. Understanding where the pain and the manifestations of it are coming from can help you forgive yourself and others. It helps restore confidence and builds a healthier self-image which will translate into a God-image and God-esteem.

Here's a list of hints on how to use your emotions as tools:

1. *Do not react on the spot.* Be aware that you are now in the business of using your emotions instead of them using you. Take some time to try to figure out what they are saying, what is the message and what is really going on here? Should you really be this fearful, hurt by rejection, angry or depressed? Ask yourself what lie or faulty perception has been planted by a previous bad experience. Is this present situation just picking the scab off an old wound?

2. *Line up with God's Word.* If your emotion is extreme and birthed out of pain, does the source of it and your reaction to it line up with the Bible? Do the emotional reactions reaffirm lies or truth about what God says about you? *If anyone is in Christ, he is a new creation; the old has gone, the new has come!* (2 Corinthians 5:17).

3. *Do not waste your pain!* It takes practice and some-
    times you will slip back into the old beliefs in your
    head, but try to become aware of your thoughts.
    You are changing some patterns and you do not
    want to miss any lessons and end up prolonging
    your healing. You need to think and do some new
    things. God would not have you waste your pain,
    so redeem it!

Let's talk about how to tell when it is right to confront an abuser.

When it is the right time sometimes action is called for
and that may mean confrontation. However, the relationship between anger and confrontation must be kept holy.

Confrontation is about the abuser(s) and anger is
about you. It is okay to be angry with what was done but
in order to confront the situation properly you must be
able to separate the sin from the sinner. That takes time
and is not easy. Be aware that anger and confrontation are
close relatives. The story in the Bible where Nathan con-
fronts David (2 Samuel 12—read the whole thing) is a
good illustration about how God uses confrontation.
Jesus Himself became angry when the temple was defiled
(Matthew 21:12). Our bodies are temples of the Holy
Spirit (1 Corinthians 6:19). If your temple (body, mind,
will and emotions) has been violated, the recounting of
your story, to bring the other person to a place of
accountability, may make you angry.

Make sure it is anger about the deed/sin and not the
thirst for revenge. If it is revenge fueling the anger, it

means forgiveness has not yet taken place and it's too early for confrontation to take place.

Unforgiveness over time festers into hate. Hate (birthed out of pain and injury) over a period of time, forms a root of bitterness and is easily provoked to aggression. This kind of root not only blocks any future attempts at forgiveness, but also can keep fueling the desire for revenge for years. It is difficult to dig up a root like this because of the relief and pleasure it brings to the pain or injury, in that it provides a renewed sense of lost power, the declaration of personal rights which have been lost.

Healing is not about blame. It is about acknowledging that you were hurt, assessing the damage and getting on with the recovery. After some healing has taken place, it is then safer and honorable to do confrontation.

You must forgive

Before you can confront you must forgive. The words of the Bible bring healing when we practice them. Forgive for your own sake so you are no longer held in bondage with bitterness and resentment.

Forgiveness of others sometimes makes forgiveness of yourself easier too. If your abuser blamed you for the abuse, the shame needs to be released.

After you have forgiven your abuser, the time finally comes to confront them about their behavior. You will have no agenda for revenge when you meet them. Vengeance belongs to God. Confrontation is to give them an opportunity to come clean before God, and even if they don't, after this meeting they have moved into a place of accountability. They can deny, or choose any number of responses, but it has now become their responsibility. You should forgive in your heart, regardless, but the person has to say more than "I'm sorry" to be in relationship.

Repentance is the action part of forgiveness (Luke 17:3).

If after confrontation the abuser is not repentant, it's possible you cannot be in relationship with them. Whether or not they change their behavior and are of contrite heart is between them and God.

I would recommend to anyone to forgive regardless of whether the abuser is dead or alive, repentant or not. Whether they repent or not will only determine if you can be in relationship with them.

Reconciliation does not always happen right away. I know that many will be angry just reading the word "reconciliation" and say things like, "There is no way!" and "If you knew what they had done, you wouldn't either!" I have heard angry talk like this before and it is okay. I say that because some of those words came out of my own mouth. At least you're honest about it. Now, be honest about how much it hurts.

This is why Jesus came; this is why He offers the example of the cross and reconciliation. He wants to stop the hurting and He wants you to have life more abundantly (John 10:10). He is the Redeemer!

As you anticipate the possibility of a healing journey you may experience some fear, hope and even nervousness in anticipation of the process. Nevertheless, after you have gone down this path, remember that joy comes in the morning. It is the experience of breakthrough!

After you have had some experience with that, you will experience a change in all your relationships, including your relationship with God. Moreover, you will experience a peace you have not known possible before. Helpless and hopeless will seem like lies from a distant past.

Personal Stories from
Survivors of Child Abuse

Changed Forever
by Dorothy Wright

As I look back over this passing decade it seems like an entire lifetime.

I recall my first cry to the Lord to help me. I had been struggling within myself to find strength, willpower or something to give me the ability to quit drinking, along with all the other harmful things that I continued doing. I would promise myself that it was all over then I'd find myself again and again in the same situation.

There I sat on the barstool, angry with myself for failing again. I cried out to God, saying, "If you are real, get me out of this mess!" Well, it wasn't long afterwards that I was out of that mess but didn't realize that it was the Lord that had saved me from myself. Another year went by before I made a step into a church or a commitment to Jesus. When I did finally go to church I watched and wondered for another year.

It was after relocating to a new town in Alberta that I seemed to really desire change like never before. I was making a new turn in my life. In our search for activities and friends we attended an evening event for children at a Pentecostal church. At that time my three beautiful children and I had made our first commitment to Jesus, our Lord and Savior.

I often found myself wishing that things could have changed instantly so that I would not have to experience growing and changing pains. However that is not realistic. The pains were to help me and shape me. When I did come to the Lord I had a lot of baggage and I needed to learn how to release things, one by one, to Jesus.

I am a First Nation Cree from the northern part of Alberta. I grew up in an alcoholic home. My mother was a child from residential school. My home life was very abusive—sexually, mentally and physically. I carried all this for as long as I could then turned to alcohol to help me along in other very destructive behavior.

Alcohol seemed to be the only thing that helped me to cope with all the pain of the abuse. It would put the emotional pain on hold. Yes, I could and would say openly that I was sexually abused and I had some very distinct memories. But I would say that it was not a big deal...I was in denial!

After I made a commitment to Jesus as my Lord and Savior I was set free from alcohol and no longer had the controlling agent over my emotions. Therefore, it was time to come out of denial and face truth and begin to deal with the sexual abuse issues in my life.

For many years of my life I have wondered what was worse— the actual incidents of abuse or the haunting memories that would replay through my mind, over and over, driving me to do the absurd things that I did. Pain and anguish would flood through my body as if the actual events were taking place. I had memories of being violated as a small girl. This violation and betrayal of trust came from people who were supposed to care for me, love me and protect me. It left me confused and very untrusting, with a big question within my life: why?

The lack of nurturing and security that took place in my childhood caused great feelings of insecurity even into my adult life. I always had feelings of unworthiness, guilt and shame. I can remember so often, sometimes even now, searching within myself for an encouraging, positive thing to hold on to. There was a strong desire to see myself past all of that darkness, to be able to look at myself in the mirror without fear of seeing myself, to be able to say that I am fearfully and wonderfully made in God's image.

With no answers for my life or for my children I was feeling totally lost after trying the systems that the world had to offer. I knew that if something didn't change history would repeat itself in the next generation. When I was desperate Jesus came into my life and set me free from addiction and the effects of all the abuse. He is still working this out in my life today.

I know that every person's experience is different. What worked for me isn't necessarily going to work for everyone. There is an answer. You can truly change! For me it started with desire; I wanted the cycle to stop—now. I couldn't bear seeing this destruction for my children and grandchildren. And after I ran out of options that the world offered, I ran to Jesus!

I totally surrendered to the Lord and was set free

from addiction, free from my desire to use substances of any kind. However, my personality or character needed help. I needed to learn this new way of living, what was right or wrong. I also needed to be in a place where I could receive that teaching, like parenting skills. I needed to know why we need fathers, or even parents for that matter. I had no basic understanding of responsibility, discipline or love. Many teachers/pastors, counselors and supportive friends have loved me and counseled me throughout this walk of healing. I can truly say that Jesus has made a way where there seemed to be no way!

There is hope for healing! I can say that today because of where I was and because of my new freedom. It hasn't been easy but with a strong support system, with people that love you and know and understand what you are dealing with, you too can make it!

The Secret
by Jim Uttley

Just prior to my tenth birthday my parents made arrangements for me to go to school many miles away. The remoteness of our home in the bush meant that I would live in a foster home in order to attend school.

Mom and Dad didn't know it at the time but those years were the worst of my life—especially the first year. For the first two weeks I cried myself to sleep a lot. I was so homesick.

I shared a room with the family's fifteen-year-old son. He was a bully—always doing things to get me into trouble. But somehow, because he was older, and because I didn't have an older brother, I looked up to him.

Shortly after my arrival something happened which was to have a profound effect on my young life and it affected me into adulthood.

It all began rather innocently. Each day after the noon meal we would take a nap until it was time to go back to school. As kids we were required to rest quietly on our beds.

One day, my roommate, while lying on his bed, exposed his genitals and began playing with them. I was shocked. A day or so later he ordered me over to his bed and showed me, in detail, what he was doing. I found it repulsive but felt that if I didn't obey it would mean trouble for me.

That was just the beginning. From there it continued until he was forcing me to participate in activities including oral sex and, on a couple of occasions, even attempted anal intercourse.

All this sickened me but I also felt trapped. If I were to tattle on him his parents would never believe me. It seemed he always won out in any confrontation.

I soon learned that this fellow's sexual escapades weren't limited to our bedroom but that he shared his "talents" with some other kids who were also older than I was.

One afternoon, after a swim in our swimming hole, the older guys abruptly sent some of us younger boys home. My buddies and I hurried off. Suspicious about why we couldn't stay, we circled around and came back to hide in the bushes about 20 feet away. We couldn't believe our eyes. The older fellows were standing around in a circle masturbating together, making a game out of it. I learned years later that some of these fellows were involved in other sexual feats led by my roommate.

My buddies and I never breathed a word of this to anyone. We were under a "death threat" not to speak about it. I had been severely warned by my roommate that if I shared what went on in our bedroom he would "kill me." I took it literally because I saw what he could do on other occasions.

I kept the secret hidden for over 30 years.

How did all of this affect my life? What did that year of sexual and physical abuse do to me? It gave me a warped view of what really makes a man. I was uncomfortable around other men, especially strong, authoritative men. I found them intimidating.

Finally, at the suggestion of a friend, I got up the courage to see a counselor. I didn't tell anyone, not even my wife. I went for about six weeks and found it helpful. But it was only the first step.

Another step was to tell my parents and share with them this secret that I kept hidden all these years. They were deeply hurt. My mother told me that if they had known what was happening they would have taken me out of that home immediately.

Perhaps the best result was that I was able to make

contact with my abuser after 30 years. I told him I forgave him for the abuse and trauma he put me through. I asked him to forgive me for all the anger and bitterness I held inside against him, causing me so much pain. He said he forgave me. I felt like a huge weight was lifted from my shoulders. He told me he was sorry for the pain he had caused. He went on to say that an adult had also abused him when he was 12.

Unfortunately, I don't know where this fellow is in his relationship with the Lord. Only God knows how he has dealt with these compulsions in his own life. I also had opportunity to discuss those events with other childhood friends who were there. They shared how their lives had been negatively affected by this fellow's actions. Just this interaction with them has been freeing.

Times have definitely changed since the late fifties and early sixties. It is doubtful that my abuser would have been sued and brought to trial for his actions back then. Today people can be taken to court for even the suggestion of sexual assault. People in those days didn't take people to court for even the vilest of sexual acts against children. Some would have if they could, but people just didn't talk about such things back then.

The only chance that legal steps would be taken against my abuser would have been if I had accused him and someone would have believed me. Or if my father or another adult were to catch him in the act and report it.

As I think back to that October day in '59, when my roommate proceeded to abuse me, I ask myself, "What escape windows did I have? Were there any? Or did I really want to see and feel what was happening—the thrill of progression towards an uncertain, yet enticing end?"

I had to admit to myself that there might well have been things that I could have done to prevent this from happening or to change the circumstances. But as a ten-year-old boy living in a strange house with people I had known for just a couple months, what might have been the right thing to do, was also that which seemed the most impossible.

For anyone who has experienced similar situations—don't hide it or keep it to yourself. Find someone you can trust to share the story with. Get counseling if necessary. But please, don't cover it up. In the end you will be spared a lot of hurt, pain and false guilt.

Thirty Years Shrunk Into One Day
by Barb Wolfe

I never knew my dad and lost my mom when I was just a baby on a Saulteaux reserve in Lestock, Saskatchewan. I was placed in a foster home where I suffered a lot of pain. I never felt that I belonged to the family. I was mistreated and picked on a lot and always made to feel like the "black sheep." I was sexually abused by a member of my foster family during the 16 years I was there.

When I was 16 I was moved to Saskatoon to attend a school for young people with special needs. My life began to change directions a year later in 1984 when I accepted Jesus Christ into my heart. At age 19 I started attending Key-Way-Tin Bible Institute, a Bible school for Native people in Lac La Biche, Alberta. In 1993 I moved to Winnipeg and received Christian counseling to deal with the abuse I had experienced while I was growing up. I received a lot of healing from the Lord as I released the pain I had tried to suppress all those years.

However, I came to realize that for 30 years I had been carrying emotional baggage because of the attachment I still had with my mom's death. Even though she had died when I was just a 9-month-old baby, I was still living with the aftermath of rejection and depression.

There was a cemetery right behind the house I used to live in. Every other day I used to go for a walk there until this one day I spotted a tree along the riverbed. I claimed that tree as my spot where I would come to rest, listen to music, read, cry and meditate. The reason I spent a lot of time in the cemetery was because of the need to feel close to my mom. This strong attachment came from not having the opportunity to put her to rest when she died. It created a longing to do what I had missed doing and that was to say goodbye. When Mother's Day came I would go to the cemetery and pay my respects to my mother. Even though she was absent in body she was never far from my heart.

On September 23, 1998, I had the privilege to drive more than six hours with a friend to my mom's home reserve in Lestock to properly say goodbye and pay my respects to my beloved mother, Violet Wolfe. She was only 32 years old when she passed away. We arrived at the Band office where we were directed to Mary and Georgina who had been friends with my mom. They shared some personal recollections with me. I also met my mom's brother Matthew—an uncle I never knew I had—and visited with him for a while.

The final moment came when I was directed to the home church cemetery that was located about a mile out of town. I felt the need to put on my moccasins. I walked in the grave yard and I found what I believed to be the site where mom was buried. I knelt down to put flowers on the grave site. I began to read to my mom from a book called "I'll Love You Forever" by Robert Munsch. The book is basically about a son who looked after his mother when she was sick because this was the example she had set when he was growing up.

I felt that the time had come for me to read that story out loud to her and express feelings that, even though she had died when I was only 9 months old, I still loved her and forgave her for leaving me behind. As I read some parts of the book I began to laugh; at other times I cried. As I finished the story I felt the need to release my mother back to the Great Creator.

As I was praying I lifted my hands and face and I felt God's presence at the deepest part of my grieving. I felt that He was drying my tears as He brought cleansing and healing to my emotions. As God's light healed me on the inside it felt like the sun was shining on my face. After that, I lay on the ground beside the grave and I felt comforted because the Great Creator was taking care of me. As I left the cemetery I felt that I had made my peace with my mom and that she knew I was in the hands of the Great Creator.

It was a long drive there and a long drive back but it was worth it. I had to be willing to take the journey to a hard place so that I could receive my healing. I wanted to tell the story of how 30 years of my life were shrunk into one day to encourage others to take their journeys and find their own healing. For some it might be a journey to a distant place; for others it is a journey to a distant memory but for all it is a journey that is necessary.

Facts and Fiction About Child Abuse, by Dr. Nancy Faulkner - reprinted from the *User's Guide for The Niktinaht Chronicles,* A National Film Board of Canada release. Used with permission.

Good Kids Make Good Victims, (c) Focus on the Family, Colorado Springs, Colorado. Used with permission. All rights reserved.

How to Raise a Sex Offender, National Clearing House on Family Violence, Health and Welfare Canada.

Survivors of Abuse by Phil E. Quinn, reprinted from *Renegade Saint.* (c) 1986. Published by Abingdon/Cokesbury Press. Used with permission.

CHAPTER THREE

Do the Effects of
Fetal Alcohol Syndrome
Still Haunt You?

THE WORTH OF A CHILD

Children are one of the greatest joys of life. Children had great value to Native people in the past. Children were their only connection with the future. They sacrificed much for their children. They worked hard to prepare them for life...children were their pride and joy. But today children too often are aborted, abandoned and neglected. Wise parents know their children are of great worth. Each child is a complete person, not just half of a person on the way to becoming a whole person. Often adults expect children to act like grownups. This is not the best way to help a child grow up. Good parents respect a child for being a complete person already.

Parents will show respect for a child by not insulting him as they correct him for making a mistake. The child is not a bad person because he did a bad thing. He is a good person who did a bad thing.

Parents should make a child feel that he is worth something. They should be careful not to make fun of him when they speak to him or correct him. When a child is corrected he should be spoken to as a person who should do better. He needs to be carefully taught just what is expected. If he disobeys because he wants to disobey he should be corrected in such a way that would correct what he did wrong. He should never be corrected in anger.

Parents can also show respect to a child by playing with him—playing his games and enjoying the things he enjoys. They should give a child freedom to say things the way he understands. Parents need to listen to him talk and show him that what he says is understood. They must remember that a child has feelings too. He has hopes and dreams about his life and future. Good parents will understand that the position of the child in the family is important. The child's position affects the way the child feels about himself.

In general, the oldest child often is a leader. The second oldest child often becomes a follower. It quite often happens, too, that the youngest child becomes "spoiled" by the parents and older brothers and sisters. A spoiled child is one who is given special privileges and attention beyond what the other children receive.

There is sometimes a danger of one of the middle children being tempted to feel like the "black sheep" (the one who does not belong) in the family.

Black sheep are formed, not born. They are usually the ones who feel left out, who get the "dirty work" to do in the family. They get more of the blame than the other children when things go wrong. This will cause the feeling of bitterness and the bad behavior, which gives them the black sheep name.

One of the quickest ways to destroy a child's personality and self-worth is to make fun of what he says. He will soon get the message that no one wants him as he is. Soon he will learn to have no respect for himself. He will either fight and cause trouble or he will withdraw and become depressed, even suicidal.

Each child is a special design made by God.

Your hands put me together and made me... (Job 10:8).

Each child has a special job and special place in life that no one else can fill. Parents have the opportunity to help their child to grow and to become the special kind of person that God wants him to be. Many children do not seem to understand that they are special.

One of the most common complaints of children and teenagers is, "I wish I were someone else." If a child thinks or says this, it shows that he is not feeling right about himself or at least some part of himself.

The Bible gives a warning about those who are always comparing themselves to others:

They decide what they think is good or bad and compare themselves with those ideas. They are foolish (2 Corinthians 10:12).

Each child in the family needs special encouragement from his father and mother. He needs a continual reminder that he is of great worth. Fathers and mothers need to help their child learn good inward qualities of love, kindness, honesty, determination and so on. These qualities will stay with the child all his life and help him to feel the special place God has for him.

Each child needs help to look at life from God's point of view as written in the Bible.

> ...*A man looks at what a person looks like on the outside, but the Lord looks at the heart* (1 Samuel 16:7).

CONDEMNING CHILDREN
NOT YET CONCEIVED

by Jim Uttley

During the summer of 1996, the story of a young Aboriginal woman's tragic addiction to sniff was printed and broadcast across Canada. The woman, although in the mid-stages of pregnancy, refused to get treatment despite the threat that her addiction was endangering the life of her unborn child. The debate focused on individual rights versus societal rights; the rights of the unborn versus a woman's right to choose or reject treatment for her drug addiction.

On August 13, 1996, Justice Perry Schulman released his decision. In giving his judgment he was careful to say that it was not based on "fetal rights" but on the fact that the woman was "mentally incompetent." Although the judge did not refer to fetal rights, he did include the suggestion that the law should include the rights of the unborn child when the mother decides to carry her fetus to term.

The decision forced the woman into treatment. An appeal was made and Schulman's decision was overturned.

This woman's case was argued before the Supreme Court of Canada. Winnipeg Child and Family Services took the stand that a fetus does have established legal rights. They cite this example. A person can sue for injuries inflicted before birth. An example of this is a lawsuit filed on behalf of a baby who was injured in a car accident before birth.

This Native woman's case began during her fourth pregnancy. She had already given her three other children to government care. Two of them are mentally and physically handicapped as a result of her drug abuse.

We agree with those who took this case to the Supreme Court of Canada. Unborn children do have rights. These rights must be protected especially when an expectant mother is, through her actions, endangering her life and the life of her unborn child. (The woman eventually won her Supreme Court case.)

This woman's story, tragic as it is, is not unique. It is repeated hundreds of times in North America. Women willfully or unwillingly have sex, conceive and all the while refuse to give up alcohol or drugs for the sake of their unborn child. In many cases these mothers are unable to quit. They need someone else to make that decision for them. The results of their willful drinking or drug addiction has produced tragic results.

It is currently estimated that every year in the United States and Canada over 12,000 babies are born with full Fetal Alcohol Syndrome (FAS) and another 80,000 with Fetal Alcohol Effect (FAE). Another 350,000 babies are bombarded with illegal drugs before they are born. Studies show that crack cocaine causes learning defects similar to alcohol.

These children are born with a full range of problems. Some have seizures, bodily defects, or poor coordination, sight and hearing. And that's only half the story.

There is nothing that will restore these babies to who

they might otherwise have been. These mothers and their partners want freedom to make their own choices as to their sexual activities, often producing children for whom they don't want to take responsibility. However, with freedom, comes responsibility.

Some would debate that we have only recently become aware of the dangers of drinking while being pregnant. This is false. The early Greeks and Romans knew better. In Carthage, the bridal couple was forbidden from drinking wine on their wedding night in order that defective children might not be conceived. In an 1834 report to the British House of Commons a select committee investigating drunkenness indicated that infants born to alcoholic mothers sometimes had "a starved, shriveled and imperfect look." In 1900 there were reports of increased abortion and stillbirth rates among chronic alcoholic women and an increased frequency of epilepsy in their surviving offspring.

Sounds like we've known for hundreds of years about the dangers of taking alcohol and drugs when pregnant.

In a survey taken during the 1980s it was found that Native Americans far surpassed all other ethnic groups in the number of children born with FAS/E. This is mind boggling and very frightening.

A New York City Health Department official estimated that births to drug-abusing mothers had increased in New York City by about 3,000 percent in the past 10 years. What will our societies be like in the next five to ten years when these children become young adults and become parents? Will they repeat the tragic addictions of their parents? Research gives more than enough evidence that they will.

The efforts of organizations such as Mothers Against Drunk Driving (MADD) have been quite successful in cutting down the number of accidents caused by drunk drivers. Who or what organization is going to cut down on the birth of FAS babies?

Michael Dorris, the late author and spokesman on behalf of FAS children, wrote these emotional words in 1990:

> *If we close our eyes we condemn children not yet even conceived to preordained existences of sorrow and deprivation, governed by prison, victimization and premature death...we worry about the very fabric of society when hundreds of thousands of others...become teenagers, become adults, in the year 2000.*

A RANSOMED HOPE
by Matthew Suriano

We have all seen smiling children, children whose happiness and innocence make us long to protect them. But for children suffering from FAS it is too late to protect them from the damage done to their minds and bodies because of their mother's alcohol drinking. Their smiling faces will look a little bit different. A child born with FAS will have a head that seems much smaller than the rest of his body. His eyes will be set too far apart above the flat wide area of his upper lip.

Alcohol is a teratogen, or teratogenic agent. This means "relating to, or causing developmental malformations and monstrosities" and is taken from the Greek word "teras" which means "monster." In FAS, we do not see monsters but rather children who will grow up having no chance for a normal life because of what happened to them before they were born. Many people suffer in FAS/E but the real victims are the children that are born with this affliction. The casualties are the hope and promise that comes with every newborn child. The tragedy is that nothing can be done to correct the damage already inflicted upon them.

According to the Surgeon General of the United States (Department of Health and Human Services, 1981), no amount of alcohol consumed by a pregnant woman can be considered "safe." As little as two drinks a day can put the child at risk for a number of different symptoms. Studies have shown that even 100 grams a week (roughly the size of a Dixie cup) can affect the size of the child (Dorris, 1989). The most dangerous form of drinking is "binge drinking" which can cause more brain damage to the unborn child than drinking the same amount during a drawn-out period.

Researchers have developed a system of identification that requires three characteristics to be evident in a child before they are diagnosed as FAS. The areas that the researchers look for in possible FAS victims include: behavioral disorder or mental disorder; small size; facial abnormalities. Even when not enough symptoms are evident a person may still be diagnosed as FAE or Fetal Alcohol Exposure, a condition that is generally without the presence of physical problems and usually does not occur until the child has reached his or her teenage years. The dangers of these classifications are that the process to identify children with FAS/E is still relatively new and many people who suffer from these conditions go undiagnosed.

Binge drinking has been linked to facial defects found in FAS. Researchers have also found that facial defects are often the result of exposure to alcohol during the first three months of pregnancy, especially during the first two months.

When a woman drinks alcohol during the first three months after conception, she is exposing her unborn baby to a teratogen at a time when the major organs are being developed (Coles, 1994). The growth of a child is affected by the mother's drinking of alcohol during all stages of the pregnancy but especially so during the first and third trimester.

Even a little bit of alcohol consumed on a weekly basis during the first three months can put the child at risk of being undersized. The size of the head and brain is one of the most lasting results of growth impediment due to alcohol damage occurring in the first three months. Often, children with the most distinct facial signs of FAS are the most severely affected in behavior and intellect. A woman may take a drink, not knowing she has conceived, and permanently damage her unborn child for life. Children affected by fetal alcohol syndrome exhibit physical, mental and behavioral disabilities. Smaller height and weight, physical abnormalities, hyper-activity, learning difficulties, developmental delay or motor and behavioral problems are also caused by the exposure of unborn babies to alcohol.

The child's eyes are small and spaced too far apart. A flap of skin folds across the corners of his eyelids, known as "epicanthic folds." Research indicates poor vision, a common symptom of FAS, results from alcohol consumption during the third to sixth month of pregnancy. Alcohol causes the lenses and corneas to become mis-shapen and the optical nerves to become underdeveloped. The effects of damaged sensory organs in FAS cases can last well past adolescence and possibly be permanent.

An FAS child is extremely small. He is short in stature, extremely thin and "small boned." His condition is termed by researchers as "failure to thrive." No matter how well he is fed and regardless of how much he exercises, he will be undersized throughout his childhood. Steady consumption of alcohol increases the risk and the seriousness of FAS/E. It has been clinically shown that children of mothers who quit drinking during the fourth to sixth month are smaller at birth and have lower intelligence ratings than the children of mothers who quit drinking during their first three months. FAS children often experience problems growing in behavior as well as in body. Along with failure to thrive, many FAS children experience problems walking and talking. The child is never safe while the mother drinks during pregnancy.

FAS/E children experience behavioral problems ranging from hyperactivity to mental retardation because alcohol slows down the brain's development. When a pregnant woman drinks alcohol she is exposing her unborn child to one of the top causes of mental retardation in the world. Research shows us that alcohol slows down the central breathing activity of the fetus through its initial effect on the brain. Alcohol can have a permanent effect on the outer layer of the brain as well as on the senses (touch, taste, sight, and hearing).

What this means is that children will suffer from a long list of mental and behavioral setbacks. Due to alcohol's effect on the brain the FAS child will show difficulty in movement and balance. He or she will tend to have a limited attention span, will be impulsive, and won't be afraid to do what other children are normally hesitant to do.

Despite the fact that some FAE children tend to talk a lot, the FAS/E child may also show poor verbal understanding and speech disorders.

Delays in bodily growth are one of the most commonly seen symptoms in FAS and delays in mental growth are one of the most serious and long-lasting symptoms of FAS. Together, these are the two most frequently observed symptoms of FAS.

The last three months of pregnancy are a crucial period for fetal brain development and, along with the first three months, is an extremely susceptible period in regards to the effects on physical growth. Alcoholic intake by a mother during the last third of her pregnancy, the period that is most visible, can be terribly damaging to her unborn child.

Because an adequate educational or vocational program has not been found that can fulfill the FAS/E child's needs, the child is often prone to a variety of social problems later on in life. The fine motor problems become more evident as the FAS child grows. Late adolescent FAS victims often suffer from emotional problems and high activity. With a poor IQ and poor social skills, the FAS/E child has difficulty finding his or her place in society during the teenage years and as a result has few friends, becoming isolated and lonesome.

The FAS/E teenager or adult may be prone to substance abuse and other criminal behavior and sometimes has bad sexual behavior.

Because FAS/E children grow up with their behavioral patterns and intellect not properly developed, they become poorly equipped for most types of work (Reid, 1990). FAS victims are portrayed as people who are unable or have great difficulty telling time, knowing the difference between right and wrong, and knowing how to handle money (Dorris, 1990). All these factors make it almost impossible for them to live life on their own. The burden is on their family or the government to provide for these FAS people for the rest of their lives.

They lack proper development in areas such as emotions, communication, and learning. The standard school curriculum is not suited to meet their needs. The costs of other programs is great.

A test program in California costs an estimated $15,000 per student and no educational system has yet to prove it is completely effective for FAS children (Dorris, 1990).

Dr. Anne Streissguth writes:

"No longer can FAS be viewed as just a childhood disability—the changing needs of this population must be considered as they enter the adolescent years."

Every year around 7,500 FAS babies are born into the United States. Countless more will be diagnosed as being FAE. Many of these FAS babies are Native Americans. One U.S. study showed that the chances of a child being FAS were 30 times greater for Native Americans and Alaskan Natives than white children.

The terrible fact of this "plague" is that it is entirely preventable. The children that are born to suffer in this world with FAS and FAE would have been spared had their parents stopped drinking during pregnancy.

Many of us find an easy solution in alcohol, but in life there are no "easy solutions" and the side effects of many of our easy solutions may live and affect our lives as well as our surrounding society for years to come.

FACING FAS/E
by Jane George

A raw egg congeals in a container as Janice Bedard pours rubbing alcohol over it. "This is what happens to an unborn baby's brain when a mother drinks," she says.

The small crowd gathered at the Parish Hall in Iqaluit passes around the egg. They've come here to learn more about Fetal Alcohol Syndrome (FAS) and Fetal Alcohol Effects (FAE) at the first public meeting of the Baffin Fetal Alcohol Network.

Bedard's demonstration is a graphic way of showing what happens to a fetus when a pregnant woman drinks alcohol. Alcohol can similarly damage the growing cells of the baby's body and brain.

Just as suicide once was, FAS is a hidden problem, one that is particularly hard for families to acknowledge.

"There's always denial," says Iqaluit social worker Eva Groves. Network organizer Bedard says also there's a reluctance to officially recognize the effects of FAS. Many fear stigmatizing mothers and children by such a diagnosis. "But these children are already labeled as not being bright. At least if you have a diagnosis of neurological damage, it's another thing than saying they're bad kids."

Without a diagnosis parents may also not receive the support they need in dealing with children affected by their mothers' drinking. Problems often begin to show during pre-school years. Fetal-alcohol children may be constantly in trouble or have difficulties with their peers.

Yet, some educators are slow to acknowledge FAS in schools. Apart from disciplinary action, schools have little to offer affected children. There's no extra money for special programs. Current educational practice calls for students of varying ability to be taught in the same classroom.

"I'm not a doctor," says Mary West of Iqaluit's Akuluk Daycare. "I can't diagnose it, but there's a big problem in town."

In Inuvik in the Western Arctic, where alcohol can be freely consumed in bars, researchers found that 38 percent of Inuit children in their study were affected by FAS.

One Iqaluit health worker says that she sometimes meets intoxicated women she knows are pregnant or trying to conceive. Her words of warning fall on deaf ears though. "We're beating our heads on the wall here."

The greatest damage occurs to the fetus before 8 weeks. Many women may consume alcohol before they even know they've conceived.

Even adults affected by FAS are becoming pregnant. And they, like their mothers before them, probably don't understand that their lifestyle is a threat to the welfare of their children.

Pregnant women who come to prenatal classes where time is spent discussing FAS are usually well educated Qallunaat. So, to spread the word, the Baffin Fetal Alcohol Network plans to begin distributing a bilingual pamphlet on FAS.

The Baffin Regional Treatment Centre may also become more involved in FAS awareness and prevention.

"It's an area that needs attention," says social worker Hannah Kilabuk. "With other people involved, the community can be involved. I hope it'll be successful."

SECONDARY DISABILITIES AND PROTECTIVE FACTORS

Secondary Disabilities are those that a person with FAS/E is not born with and that could probably be improved through better understanding and practical help. These disabilities were studied through a life history interview that was given to all available caretakers/informants of 415 individuals with FAS/E who ranged in age from 6 to 51 years.

1. Mental health problems were by far the most prevalent secondary disability experienced by over 90% of the full sample.

2. Disrupted school experience (defined as having been suspended or expelled from school or having dropped out of school) was experienced by 60% of the clients (12 years and over).

3. Trouble with the Law (defined as having been in trouble with authorities, charged, or convicted of a crime) was experienced by 60% of the clients (12 years and over).

4. Confinement (including inpatient treatment for mental health problems or alcohol/drug problems, or having been incarcerated for a crime) was experienced by about 50% of the clients (12 years and over).

5. Inappropriate sexual behavior was noted for about 50% of the clients (12 years and over).

6. Alcohol/Drug problems were noted for about 30%

of the clients (12 and over). For those who were at least 21 years of age and older, two additional secondary disabilities were identified.

7. Dependent living characterized 80% of the clients (21 and over).

8. Problems with employment characterized 80% of the clients (21 and over).

Eight factors came out that are helpful and protective in terms of secondary disabilities. In order of their strength as "universal" protective factors, they are:

1. Living in a nurturing and stable home for over 72% of life
2. Being diagnosed before the age of 6 years
3. Never having experienced violence against oneself
4. Staying in each living situation for an average of 2.8 years
5. Experiencing a good quality home from age 8 to 12 years
6. Having applied for and been found eligible for DDD
7. Having a diagnosis of FAS (rather than FAE)
8. Having basic needs met for at least 13% of life

Most of the environmental influences that appear to be helpful for people with FAS/E are, of course, good for all people. Most of the universal protective factors are outward so that families, communities and nations have an opportunity to do something about them.

FETAL ALCOHOL EFFECTS

Fetal Alcohol Effects (FAE) is an unclear term that people use in many different ways. Usually the term is used to describe children who have one or two of the characteristics of FAS. Experts do not recommend using the term FAE because there are not set rules for identifying FAE and because many of the symptoms of FAE can be caused by things other than drinking during pregnancy. Experts think it's better to tell parents, caregivers, or professionals about the specific symptoms that the child is experiencing instead of labeling them FAE or FAS. The results of physical, psychological and behavioral tests are better for making decisions about special programs or services that the person needs.

It's hard to diagnose FAS for many reasons:

- There is no one symptom that can identify FAS.
- There are no accepted tests to diagnose FAS.
- Many FAS symptoms change as the child gets older.
- FAS symptoms are hard to see in babies.
- It is hard to know how much alcohol the mother drank.

It is important to remember that the symptoms of FAS could also be the symptoms of other problems. For this reason, all other causes of physical and behavioral problems have to be ruled out before the child can be diagnosed with FAS.

I Was Beyond Human Help
by Paul Morehead as told to Sherry Turner

At four years of age I was taken away from my birth mother and forced to stay with strangers. I didn't know why I could not live with my mother. A lady came and took me to a place I had never been to before, then just left me there. Nobody told me what was going on.

The first four years of my life had been drastic. My mother was an alcoholic—but I loved her. I remember being really hungry one time and there was no food in the house. She pushed me away and continued to drink. Although I didn't know it then, she needed alcohol more than she needed food. All I knew was that I was hungry and she rejected me. I was hurt and, little did I know it, it would affect me the rest of my life.

I was born with Fetal Alcohol Syndrome (FAS). Back then not much was known about it and since my case was not severe, no one knew I had it. More recent research shows that anything less than a full-blown case of FAS is sometimes called Fetal Alcohol Effects (FAE). That is what I have since most of my physical features are normal. The main effects I have are thinking disorders which include bad judgment and not being able to learn from my mistakes.

It was in my best interest that I was taken away and made to live with strangers. They were good to me and loved me. They took me to church every Sunday. Yet I was so afraid to get close to them; I didn't want them to reject me like my mother had. Also, being an Indian, I didn't feel like I belonged. I always counted on going back to my real mother just as soon as she could quit drinking.

When I was seven years old I was told my mother had died. I would live with my foster family the rest of my life because now they had adopted me. When I learned my mother had died I was so mad at her! Blame was a big part of my life. I blamed her for dying on me. I blamed her for not keeping me. I blamed her for not giving me a chance to know my heritage and relatives and not being able to grow up in Indian culture where I belonged.

Why did she have to die on me? Didn't she know I was waiting so desperately to go back to live with her? I made a vow to myself not to get close to anyone so they couldn't hurt me as badly as my mother had.

I graduated from high school and went on to graduate from a vocational school. It was then that I started drinking. I was fired from my first job because of it. I talked with a counselor who encouraged me to attend an Alcoholics Anonymous (AA) meeting. Being told I was an alcoholic was devastating for me. All I could think about was my mother and how she drank and wasn't able to take care of me. I thought about how messy our house always was. I didn't want a life like that. If I was an alcoholic, then that's how it might be for me. So I was in denial and concluded I wasn't an alcoholic.

I decided to join the Navy and was stationed in Japan. I continued to drink. After getting drunk a few times I thought I better go to one of those AA meetings just to make sure I wasn't an alcoholic. I didn't feel comfortable there because I was still in denial. I was given a drug to help me quit drinking. While on the drug, I still continued to drink. That was a deadly combination. I ended up in the hospital under the supervision of a Christian counselor. When he realized what I was doing he immediately requested that I be taken off the drug saying he didn't want to be responsible for my death. He asked me one day, "If you ever saw a demon possessed person would you cast out the demon?" I laughed, thinking this guy must be crazy. He said, "Don't laugh at God's prophet; it could happen to you."

I was discharged from the Navy because of my drinking. I went back to the United States and got on a bus. A demon possessed guy was preaching to a lady about Satan. I'd never seen anything like that! I'd been listening to the radio through headphones but had shut it off. Satanic music supernaturally came over my headphones. Was it really happening? The thing I laughed about? It was the demon possession just like the Christian counselor asked me about. I thought of what the Bible said about Jesus casting out demons. So I said to myself, prayerfully, "In the name of Jesus, shut up!" The guy couldn't talk any more and the music quit. Everything was quiet. God proved to me that day that He is real! I knew then that God isn't just some fictitious character to worship on Sundays.

For a period of time I forgot about God, was in and out of treatment centers and landed in jail. I was given a drug for depression so I could cope with life.

After getting out of jail, I decided there was no hope for me and planned to go to a reservation and drink myself to death. I sold a three hundred-dollar bicycle and started drinking with a friend.

I met a girl that night and decided to stay with her, letting my friend go to the reservation alone. A week later I found out that he got arrested for drugs and landed in the state penitentiary.

One night while drinking with my girlfriend, I blacked out, awaking to find myself at a halfway house. For the first time I realized it was my own fault and I had to do something about it myself.

I contacted my adoptive parents for the first time in over eight years. As I was talking with my dad I realized something very important. I said to him, "It's not in a treatment center where changes have to be made; it's living out here in the real world."

Each of the treatments I had been through were steps up for me. I needed all of them to get where I am today. Someone had challenged me by saying, "You didn't ask for this disease or FAE, but you have them, so what are you going to do about it?" A Christian friend told me I was beyond human help; nobody could help except God.

I said to him, "If I'm beyond human help then you better start praying for me." I haven't had a drink since then!

I had made a mess of my life. I had no money. I had no job. I was an alcoholic Indian with FAE and didn't know where to turn. Then I got a phone call from my adoptive dad asking if I'd come home for a family reunion. I had two choices; I could stay or go. The timing of that phone call was a miracle; I was just ready to go on another drunk but instead decided to go home. I had made a good decision. Prayer works!

I went home and people at the reunion were thrilled to see me after eight years! I felt good being there. I was offered a good job.

I began attending an Assemblies of God church. After hearing several of the pastor's messages I knew that it was not enough to know about God; I had to know Him personally. During one of the altar calls I went forward to accept Jesus Christ as my Savior and Lord. At that moment I asked Him to come in and take control of my life. I knew I couldn't change my life. Only God could. He did it!

I am now able to talk with my parents about my past. I am totally honest with everyone. God has truly worked a miracle in my life and I am so thankful. It feels good to be close to people who love me.

I'm now paying my bills and in about a year I'll be debt free for the first time in my life! For the first time I am faithfully tithing; it's funny how it works but I always have money. In the past I didn't trust God with my money; I thought giving offerings was like throwing it away.

I'm not on any medications. God has totally freed me from those. I am now living each day to the fullest. Drinking has been replaced with bowling, Bible studies and movies with friends. I never dreamed I would get up at 6:00 a.m. and go to a Bible study before work! My social life is wonderful. Before I felt like I didn't fit in being an Indian. Now I'm proud to be who I am and fit in perfectly with Indians or whites!

If anyone truly submits to God, He will work miracles. And it's never too late to start over! My mission is to let that be known as my life is a living testimony to that fact! IT'S NEVER TOO LATE TO START OVER! Trusting God is where it's at.

List of writers and contributors to the topic of Fetal Alcohol Syndrome:
Jim Uttley – editor Indian Life
Paul Morehouse as told to Sherry Turner
Jane George – *Nunatsiaq News*. Reprinted with Author's permission.
Ann P. Streissguth, Helen M. Barr, Julia Kogan, Fred L. Bookstein – University of Washington School of Medecine, Department of Psychiatry and Behavioural Sciences. Taken from *Understanding the Occurrence of Secondary Disabilities in Clients with Fetal Alcohol Syndrome (FAS) and Fetal Alcohol Effects (FAE)*
Northern Youth Ministries – excerpts from *The Worth of a Child.* Used with permission. Taken from *Indian Life,* Vol 18-No. 1, June-July, 1997

List of References to Bibliography:

Abel, E. (1987). Fetal alcohol syndrome and Fetal alcohol effect. (pp. 100-147). New York: Plenum Press.

Coles, C. (1984). Critical periods for prenatal alcohol exposure. Alcohol Health & Research World. 18(1),22-19.

Dorris, M. (1989). The Broken Cord.* (pp. 152-153). New York: Harper & Row.— (1990), June 25). A Desperate Crack Legacy. *Newsweek.* p. 8.

Duimstra, C., Johnson D., Kutsch D., Wang, B., Zentner, M., Kellerman, S., & Welty, D. (1993). A fetal alcohol syndrome surveillance project in American Indian communities in the northern plains. *Public Health Reports.* 108(2), 225-229.

FDA Drug Bulletin. (1981). Surgeon General's advisory on alcohol and pregnancy. (DHHS Publication No. HF!-22). Rockville, Maryland: U.S. Government Printing Office.

Gibbons, B. (1992, February). Alcohol, the legal drug. *National Geographic.,* p. 19.

Jones, J.L. & Smith D.W. (1973). Recognition of the fetal alcohol syndrome in early infancy. The Lancet 1. 1000.

Reid, D. (1990, June). Fetal alcohol effect. *Adoption Forum.* pp.1-2.

Steinmetz, G. (1992, February). Fetal alcohol syndrome. *National Geographic.* pp.37-38.

Streissguth, A.P. (1994). A long-term perspective of FAS. *Alcohol Health & Research World.* 18(1). pp. 75-59.

West, J. (eds). (1986). *Alcohol and brain development.* New York: Oxford University Press.

*an excellent book on FAS/FAE

CHAPTER FOUR

Does the Call of Gambling
Still Lure You?

WOLVES IN SHEEP'S CLOTHING
by Jim Uttley

Gambling has become a principal pastime for most North Americans. Over 160 million people in North America participate in some form of gambling. In 1996 over three hundred billion dollars were wagered in lotteries and casinos across the United States and Canada. Legalized gambling is fast becoming prevalent in Native America as well. Over 180 American Indian communities operate casinos or gaming parlors on reservations in 27 States.

Gambling is exciting. No one will deny that there is a thrill in the roll of a dice, a "good hand" or the spin of a fortune wheel. The competitive drive in all of us, together with the fascination of taking a risk, makes gambling very entertaining.

Gambling is also a big moneymaker. When the Niagara Falls, Ontario casino opened, the operators boasted that they would take in over $650 million in revenue during their first year. They accomplished that goal and surpassed it.

The gaming industry is also becoming a major employer. Hundreds of casinos across the country employ thousands of people. This says nothing of the thousands employed in hotels, restaurants and nightclubs in such gambling hot spots as Las Vegas and Atlantic City. This is one of the principle reasons cited by Native tribal officials seeking to open casinos on their reservations. One tribal leader stated that

> *"Casinos are the only economic program that has worked for Native Americans; it has worked where other government programs have failed."*

We do not deny that gambling is exciting entertainment. And we can't argue that it is making millions for tribal organizations and reservations. We also won't disagree that it has created hundreds of jobs.

The problem is that gambling is a dangerous business. Along with it comes not only economic growth and development but also social and financial problems. The gaming industry is also creating political problems for Indian bands. Many tribal leaders fear a loss of their traditional values and an increase in crime and the coming of organized crime.

Moses Okimaw, legal adviser to the Assembly of First Nations, as quoted in *McLean's* magazine, May 30, 1994, says,

"One quick result of sudden crime is that we are now hearing of rich, bratty Indian kids who won't go to school because they're all going to be millionaires."

First Nation leaders are also arguing over "Native sovereignty" as it relates to the gaming industry, saying that neither State, Provincial nor Federal government have control over reservations and therefore they have no right to control casinos.

Gambling is also devastating and ruining lives: it can be deadly!

A lot of information and statistics ought to and will sadden you. While some are becoming rich, others' lives are being destroyed. Are the economic benefits worth the cost to human lives and society? At a recent conference on problem gambling it was reported that the cost for counseling and treatment programs for gambling addicts is skyrocketing and State and Provincial governments are having to budget more money each year for gambling treatment programs.

Why are our governments turning to gambling at breakneck speed? One social observer commented that governments have taken hold of gambling in such a big way because they don't have any solutions to the problems facing society. Instead of raising taxes to cover their bills they have come up with lotteries. Although it is a form of taxation it also pacifies the people.

According to Dr. Tony Evans, the lottery is

"the most pervasive and frequently used form of gambling by ordinary people. It is one of the most exploitative gambling mechanisms in existence today."

In his book, *Tony Evans Speaks Out On Gambling & The Lottery* (Moody Press), Evans explains that in order for you to win, someone else must lose. He states that that's the nature of illegitimate gambling.

"You have to take from one to give to another. You have to make many into losers in order to have a handful of winners take everything. Every day America has mega millions of losers so a few can win. That's exploitation."

What's worse is that lotteries are designed for and financed by the poor. The majority of lottery outlets are located in poor areas. Evans states that

"...many people who make $10,000 or less a year spend up to one-fifth of their income on the lottery. If a con man were bilking poor people out of one-fifth of their income, the community would call for his head. But here is the government doing the same thing, and we call it a game."

It is time for our leaders to examine what is happening to our people. Are the economic benefits worth the cost in social devastation? If you are a gambler you need to consider how your gaming activities are affecting your life and your family. Read about this issue carefully and consider the consequences. Failure to do so could bring harm to you or someone you love.

Your Money or Your Life?
by Dr. Tony Evans

This is a serious issue because more than one hundred million North Americans gamble on some level. Three hundred billion dollars a year are spent on gambling. Whether it is playing cards in a friend's home, voting in a casino or buying a lottery ticket at the corner market, gambling touches all of us at some point.

Let me make a couple observations.

Observation number one: God is not against wealth per se. Deuteronomy 8:18 says that it is God who gives the ability to become wealthy. In 1 Chronicles 29:12-14, David praised God because "riches and honor" come from Him. Of course, God is extremely interested in how you acquire your wealth and how you handle it (1 Timothy 6:17). But God does not condemn the legitimate acquisition of wealth. To be poor is not necessarily to be more spiritual. God has no problem with you doing better this year than you did last year.

Observation number two: God encourages risk-taking, or to use a more comfortable term, investing. In Matthew 25:14-30, Jesus tells the story of a man who left his money with three of his servants to invest. If you know the story you know that the master commended the first two servants who had invested wisely and doubled his money. But think of the risks they must have taken to get that kind of return. The third servant buried his money. No risk there. He played it absolutely safe yet the master condemned him saying, "How dare you take what does not belong to you and not make more with it? The least you should have done was put it in the bank and make me some interest."

Did you know there are many Christians who are not taking legitimate risks? They have never taken the time, talents and treasure God has given them and maximized these gifts because they are too scared of the risks involved in going all out for Christ. The church needs more legitimate risk-takers. So it appears that God has no problem with wealth and He has no problem with risk-taking per se.

The first question we need to ask is, "Is your risk-taking motivated by greed?" Answering this one will go a long way to putting the issue of gambling into perspective.

One Sunday morning a man came to church looking very sad and despondent. The pastor noticed him and asked: "Why are you so sad?"

"Well, two weeks ago my uncle died and left me $75,000. Then a week ago my aunt died and left me $50,000."

The pastor said, "Wait a minute. Two weeks ago your uncle died and left you $75,000. Last week your aunt died and left you $50,000. Why are you so sad?"

The man answered, "Because nobody died this week."

Greed is a consistent desire to have more or demand the best without regard to need. The greedy person always says, "I want more."

The opposite of greed is contentment. First Timothy 6:5b-10 is one of the best statements on greed and contentment in the Bible. Notice verse 6:

Godliness actually is a means of great gain, when accompanied by contentment.

Then Paul goes on to explain that when we leave this place our wallets stay here. Therefore, a consuming desire to get rich can only lead to…

temptation and a snare and many foolish and harmful desires which plunge men into ruin and destruction (v. 9).

Then we read the verse that is so often misunderstood:

For the love of money is a root of all sorts of evil (v. 10).

Greed is not necessarily tied to how much you have. You can be rich and greedy, poor and greedy, middle-class and greedy because the heart of greed is the desire for more. I don't mean it's wrong to want a better house or a newer car or any of that. But if you cannot be content with where you are until (or unless) God takes you where you want to be, you are greedy.

God condemns greed, the lust for money. People who are greedy are susceptible to get-rich-quick schemes. The Bible clearly condemns such schemes. Proverbs 21:5 says,

The plans of the diligent lead surely to advantage, but everyone who is hasty comes surely to poverty.

Go to Proverbs 28: 20, 22:

A faithful man will abound with blessings, but he who makes haste to be rich will not go unpunished.

*A man with an evil eye hastens after wealth, and
does not know that want will come upon him.*

You ask, "How do I know when I'm being greedy?"
Let me ask you a couple of questions. First, are you pushing
even legitimate risks to the point that they become illegitimate? For instance, are you taking unwise business risks in
search of that killer deal that will put you on easy street?
Perhaps you're pouring more money than you really need
to into things like insurance in the hope that if anything
happens, you'll clean up. These are tough questions and I
can't pretend to answer them for you. God can show you
when you've crossed the line if you want to know.

If you're either participating in State-sanctioned
gambling or want to, my second question is, why do you
want to play it? For instance, do you want to play the lottery because you want to contribute to the educational
program of your State or Province? Is your motivation to
help put more police on the street or whatever the lottery
people say will happen with the money?

Or do you want to play the lottery because the government has come up with a way for you to get rich quickly?
If that is your motivation, you have forfeited God's biblical
means to wealth because He says that those who participate in get-rich-quick schemes will not go unpunished.

Don't misunderstand. The problem is not being rich.
The problem is the greed mentality you use to get there.

Let me ask you a third question. Let's say you win
twenty million dollars in the lottery. Do you think that
winning represents God's plan for your life? Can you

honestly say you took that step in obedience to God's leading? Well, I suppose it is possible. But, if you'll pardon the pun, I'll have to say the odds are against it. What I mean is that most people who play the lottery simply grab for the pot of gold because it's there. God's leading or His plan doesn't enter the picture at that particular moment.

What's the problem with that? It means winning the lottery is not tied to anything but a thirst for wealth. It is not tied to God's leading or plan for you. It's not even tied to your needs. You are asking God to bless nothingness. You are asking Him to bless getting money for money's sake: that's greed. God won't bless it!

So let me say it again. If you are not content, then you are driven by greed. I don't mean that you shouldn't want to move forward. But God wants you to be content where you are. Until He decides to give you more He wants you to be content.

As we saw earlier in 1 Timothy 6:10, the love of money is at the root of a lot of other things that can go wrong. If you love money you will pay a high price for that affection. Many of us have met people who have a lot of money and not much of anything else, including peace of heart.

Maybe you've heard how trappers use rice inside a narrow-necked jar to catch monkeys or they put shiny aluminum foil in a box covered with a wire mesh to catch raccoons. The animals reach in and grab what they want but they can't get their hands out because they are clutching their prize. And they want the stuff so bad that they will sit there stuck and get captured rather than let go to escape.

That's how Satan uses money on us. He gets us squeezing it until we want it so much we are never going to let go. Then he can capture and enslave us.

It's like the businessman who was granted one wish by a genie. He told the genie he wanted to see the stock-market report for a year from that date so he could know ahead of time where to invest and make a killing. The genie showed the businessman the stock-market report of one year ahead. At first he was excited but then he froze in fear. On the other side of the page were the obituaries: his picture was printed there.

That's a fictitious story but you get the point. Many people have bought houses and are still working on trying to make them into homes. Others have bought cars and now they ride in them alone because they have loved money.

You may remember the famous comedian Jack Benny, legendary for being a tightwad. The joke is told that one day a man came up to Benny on the street, pointed a gun at him, and said, "Your money or your life."

Benny did not say anything. The thief repeated his demand, "Your money or your life!" Still Benny didn't answer. So the thief said, "What's the matter with you? Didn't you hear me?"

"I'm thinking about it," Benny responded.

Some of us love money that much. We are not sure whether we would rather lose our money or our lives.

A SERIOUS PROBLEM

Legalized gambling is becoming more prevalent in Native North America. With the apparent success of casinos such as Foxwoods on the Mashantucket Peqot Reserve in the state of Connecticut; Mystic Lake owned by the Sakaopee Mdewakanton Dakota Tribe in Minnesota; and the Rama Casino in Rama, Ontario, other tribes are attempting to gain permission to open casinos on their reservation land. Already, 179 American Indian communities operate casinos or gaming parlors on reservations in 17 States.

In 1988, the United States Congress passed the Indian Gaming Regulatory Act (IGRA) which requires states with legal gambling to give Indian reservations an equal right to operate commercial gambling on tribal land. States are left with uncertain authority over Indian gambling within their borders because Indian bands are sovereignties and therefore are exempt from most State controls and taxes.

In Canada, the casino craze is catching on also. Manitoba, Quebec, British Columbia and Ontario each have casinos in major cities that are taking in the profits. Now the Indian bands across the country are demanding the right to open their own casinos in order to reap profits. Some bands have already signed management agreements with Las Vegas casino operators.

One criterion required for Indian bands to meet in Ontario is that the casino's profits are to be shared among all the Province's bands. Native leaders are infuriated stating that "we feel we are being forced to fight among ourselves."

First Nations leaders are also arguing over "Native sovereignty" saying that neither Provincial nor Federal governments have jurisdiction over reserves and therefore have no right to control casinos.

> *"Already some bands have been deeply divided over the gaming issue, with elders fearing the loss of their traditional values to corruption and organized crime."* (Moses Okimaw, legal adviser to Assembly of First Nations in Ottawa from *McLean's* magazine May 30/94).

Gambling in any culture brings not only economic development but social and economic problems. Most, if not all, casinos are designed without windows or clocks so that once inside you become unaware of the passing of time. The noise and excitement holds you enthralled for many hours at a time and you eventually realize that it is extremely late, and you haven't eaten or even been home to see your family. Added to that, you have spent your paycheck or a substantial amount of money and now have no money for your rent or mortgage, for groceries or bills or anything else. Hence, we are looking at an increase in crime to pay gambling habits. We are also looking at the possibility of spousal or child abuse because you are upset at the demands your family puts upon you for financial support.

There is also the drain on government funding for those who have become addicted to gambling and need counseling: the government is now responsible to provide funds to establish more treatment centers to handle these cases.

In small communities where casinos are built to provide a boost to the economy, the presence of a casino often has many negative effects on that community. There is an increase in tourism but with that increase comes heavier traffic meaning added road repairs and maintenance, more noise, often nonstop (because casinos can be open 24 hours a day), and more risk of traffic accidents and deaths. Many small businesses hoping for increased trading are forced to shut down anyway because the tourists are there solely for the casino attraction and once inside find no reason to leave until it is time to go home.

Are you living with a gambling addict?

1. Do you find yourself constantly bothered by bill collectors?

2. Is the person in question away from home for long unexplained periods of time?

3. Does this person ever lose time from work due to gambling?

4. Do you feel this person cannot be trusted with money?

5. Does this person faithfully promise that he or she will stop gambling, begging or pleading for another chance, yet gamble again and again?

6. Does this person ever gamble longer than he or she intended to, until the last dollar is gone?

7. Does this person ever gamble to get money to solve financial difficulties, or have unrealistic expectations that gambling will bring the family material comfort and wealth?

8. Does this person immediately return to gambling to try to recover losses or to win more?

9. Does this person borrow money to gamble with or to pay gambling debts?

10. Has this person's reputation ever suffered due to gambling, even to the extent of committing illegal acts to finance gambling?

11. Have you come to the point of hiding money needed for living expenses knowing that you and the rest of the family may go without food and clothing if you do not?

12. Do you search this person's clothing or go through his or her wallet when the opportunity presents itself or otherwise check on his or her activities?

13. Do you hide his or her money?

14. Have you noticed a significant change in the gambler as his or her gambling progresses?

15. Does the person in question consistently lie to cover up or deny his or her gambling activities?

16. Does this person use guilt induction as a method of shifting responsibilities for his or her gambling activities?

17. Do you attempt to anticipate this person's moods or try to control his or her life?

18. Does this person ever suffer from remorse or depression due to gambling, sometimes to the point of threatening self-destruction?

19. Has the gambling ever brought you to the point of threatening to break up the family unit?

20. Do you feel that your life together is a nightmare?

If you are living with a compulsive gambler you will answer yes to at least six of the above questions.

What is Gambling?

It took only one dollar to lead him to spend a year begging and borrowing. His roller-coaster year ended when he stole to feed his addiction to Video Lottery Terminals (VLTs).

His year-long addiction to the armless bandits ended abruptly in November 1994 after he made the fateful decision to steal power tools from a high school, pawn them and use the money to feed VLTs.

He hadn't heard from his ex-wife for about three years. Her addiction to gambling contributed to their divorce. And then one day she called. She was desperate for money. She was in trouble because they had discovered money missing where she worked and were asking her where it went. She didn't want to borrow money to pay back the debt: she wanted money to go on the lam.

For the majority of people gambling is an exciting form of entertainment. *Webster's Dictionary* defines gambling as any act accompanied by risk of loss. Games of chance include: Video Lottery Terminals (VLT), Casinos, Bingos, Lotteries, Raffles, Tear Opens (eg. Nevada Tickets), and Race Track Betting. For others, gambling becomes their reason for existing. As more time and energy is focused on gambling, less time is spent with family or at work. When a person begins to be controlled by the need to gamble this person may need help to overcome the addiction.

Do you know anyone in this situation? Or perhaps you are in need of help yourself.

DOES GAMBLING
AFFECT YOUR FAMILY?

When there is someone in your family who has a gambling addiction it can often create serious emotional and financial hardships. Many families have broken up over gambling.

In these families, a parent may be so caught up in gambling that he or she has very little of anything left to give their spouse or children.

There is evidence to show that if a grandparent or parent has a gambling problem they will most likely pass it on to their children or grandchildren. In one study, 11.4% of those surveyed indicated that they had mothers who gambled too much in the past and 15.2% had fathers who gambled too much in the past. In an American study a link was found between parental problem gaming and gambling for those they interviewed. Subjects whose parents were problem gamblers were three times more likely to have serious gambling problems themselves than those who did not have parents who have gambled. As well, those whose grandparents had gambling problems were 12 times more likely to be problem gamblers.

Can family members tell if one of them is a gambling addict? Not very often. If someone is addicted to alcohol or drugs there are often obvious signs such as getting drunk or acting "off the wall." However, when someone can't stop gambling there are often no signs. It's true that some problem gamblers may have mood swings or spend a lot of time away from home but these signs could also be signs of another problem. The problem may be so invisible that "as gambling progresses in frequency and severity, families are often in the dark about the extent of the problem."

People who are addicted to gambling spend more and more time, energy and money on their chosen activity. Family members may not know what is going on. They just know that the gambling parent isn't there. And when he or she is at home they're not in touch with what's happening in the family.

If children are old enough they may be able to understand that there are money problems in the family. All that the young children may know is that they don't get fed as often and they're not taken care of as well as before. Families are seriously affected when the parent loses a job and they end up on unemployment or welfare.

What are some other effects of addictive gambling on the spouse and family?

The Addictions Foundation of Manitoba's *Gambling and the Family: Facilitator's Guide* cites the findings of some studies done to measure this. Here are some samples:

- 11% of wives of addicted gamblers have attempted suicide.

- 25% of children of addicted gamblers have behavior or adjustment problems related to school, drug or alcohol abuse.

- 99% of financial problems in families of addicted gamblers are directly related to gambling.

- 65% of wives of addicted gamblers gave their spouses their personal savings to gamble or pay debts; 46% gave their earnings to the gambler for the same purpose.

- 56% of wives of addicted gamblers borrowed money from friends and relatives to help finance their gambling; 54% to 76% borrowed from friends and relatives in order to meet the basic needs of their families.

- 62% of wives of addicted gamblers were harassed by bill collectors and 50% were threatened by bill collectors.

- 11% of addicted gamblers are physically abusive to their spouses and 6% are physically abusive to their children.

Over one hundred million people in North America gamble. More than 400 billion dollars are spent each year on gambling on this continent.

1. Is your risk-taking motivated by greed? Answering this one will go a long way to putting the issue of gambling into proper perspective.

2. Is your risk-taking designed to displace God as the supplier of your needs? Or to put it another way, are you using luck to try to replace providence?

3. Has your gambling displaced your productivity? Are you gambling for things you should work for?

4. Are you taking a wise or unwise risk?

5. Are you becoming addicted to your little gambling thing? Better wake up because you're a candidate for a big gambling thing.

6. Is the risk you're taking exploitative in nature? To put it another way, does it require you or someone else to manipulate and use people to pull it off?

7. Does your risk-taking help or hurt society?

8. Does it do spiritual harm to others?

9. Can what you want to do be considered legitimate fun? "I only do it for a little fun," a lot of people say about their gambling. "I'm not trying to get rich or make a pile of money so I can quit working and loaf the rest of my life."

10. Is gambling good stewardship? To be a steward means that you are a manager of somebody else's property. You own nothing.

PROBLEM GAMBLING SAME AS SUBSTANCE ABUSE

Drinking alcohol and gambling are both activities that a large number of people take part in. For example, in a survey of the Province of Alberta, it was found that 79% of Albertans drink and 91% gamble. What is not being told is that for a sizable number of people excessive alcohol use or gambling leads to a range of emotional, financial, family, or health problems.

In another survey, developed by the Addictions Research Foundation of Ontario, it is estimated that 15% or more of Albertans 12 years and older currently experience some level of problems with alcohol or other drugs (that's between 320,000 and 384,000 people). That is far too large a number.

The abuse of alcohol was recognized medically as a treatable disorder in 1956. In contrast it was not until 1980 that gambling addiction was medically defined as an "impulse control" problem. These are broadly defined as "mental disorders characterized by an irresistible impulse to perform harmful acts." As a result, gambling is generally thought of as being comparable to alcohol or drug abuse.

Until recently the only data available on problem gamblers was taken from studies of mainly men attending treatment facilities or Gamblers Anonymous in the United States. The profile taken from these studies of a "typical" client was that of a male, about 40 years old, married, employed, with an above average education. In contrast, the profile of a "typical" problem gambler taken from the 1994 Alberta study is one that could be either male or female, under age 30, non-white, unmarried, with less than a high school education and an annual household income of under $25,000.

Research in other areas has found that up to half of those in treatment for problem gambling may also have a drug or alcohol problem.

EXCITEMENT LURES TEENS

- In a 1994 study of children in grades 4, 6 and 8, reasons given for gambling included enjoyment, excitement, passing the time, winning money, and peer pressure. Other studies have determined that other than for excitement and escape, gambling may be another expression of adolescence just as sex and drugs are.

- In a 1998 survey of high school students in the Quebec City area, just over three-quarters (76%) of those who answered questions reported gambling at least once in their lives. U.S. studies have shown higher involvement, with 91% of high school students saying they had gambled at least once.

- A recent Quebec study showed that the number of youth who gamble on a regular basis is rising. According to the study, gambling rates have more than doubled since the previously mentioned Quebec study.

- In another study 86% of children in grades 4 to 6 reported that they had participated in some kind of gambling (such as lotteries, bingo, card playing, sports betting and video poker). Forty percent reported gambling at least once a week.

- Almost half of the youth in the survey reported that they have gambled spending $1 to $10 a month (49.1%). While 15.6% said they spent $11 to $50 in the same time period, some report spending larger amounts: 5.5% spent $51 to $100 and 2.5% spent $101 to $250. A few (2.5%) spent more than $250 a month on gambling.

- Young people said they got the money from various sources including jobs, allowances, and illegal activities. One study found that young gamblers who have reached the final stage of problem gambling may commit crimes such as selling drugs, shoplifting, stealing from parents or employers to get the money to gamble. Of the high school students surveyed in Quebec, a total of 8.9% committed illegal activities in order to gamble. These activities included selling drugs, stealing money from someone they live with, committing other types of stealing, working for a bookmaker or selling sports cards.

- A 1986 study in the United States revealed that 15% of the high school students surveyed admitted lying about their wins and losses, 10% used illegal means to finance their gambling and 6% were unable to repay their gambling debts. Just under 6% of those questioned considered themselves to be addicted gamblers.

- In looking at gambling among youth, here are some interesting facts learned from one survey—

- A majority of youth gambled at least once during the past year.

- Boys gamble more often than girls and students in grade 9 and 12 gamble more often than students in grade 6.

- It is not uncommon for girls to play two or more games weekly or daily and for boys to play four or more games at a weekly or daily rate.
- Although the amount of gambling by teens did not increase from 1992 to 1995, this is the first generation of youth to be exposed to widespread accessibility to gambling places and gambling advertising, and it will be important to continue checking the place gambling plays among youth.

Teen gambling danger signals:
- Do you find gambling to be the most exciting activity you do?
- Do you often spend your free time involved in gambling activities?
- Do you prevent family and friends from knowing how much or how often you gamble?
- Do your friends gamble?
- Do you often daydream about gambling?
- Do you often gamble during lunch breaks, after school hours or on weekends?
- Do you miss school or other key events due to gambling activities?
- Do you often dream of solving your problems by making a big win?
- Do you ever lie about your gambling? For example, do you ever tell people that you did not gamble or that you won money when in fact you lost money?
- Have you ever argued with others because of gambling?

- Do you feel people look up to you when you win?
- Do you find that gambling allows you to "get attention" from others?
- Do you ever borrow money to gamble?
- Do you ever gamble with money that is supposed to be used for another purpose (such as lunch, the bus or clothes)?
- Have you ever stolen money from family, friends or employers or shoplifted in order to gamble or pay gambling debts?
- Do you believe that gambling is a fast and easy way to earn money?
- Do you get upset or irritable if you're unable to gamble?
- Do you most want to gamble when you're under stress?
- Do you often feel depressed or guilty because you lost money gambling?
- Is it hard for you to stop gambling after you lose money?
- Do you return to gambling after losing money in order to win it back?
- When you win, do you want to return to gamble as soon as possible because you believe that you will continue winning?
- Do you often gamble longer than intended and lose more money than intended?
- When you are gambling, do you lose track of time and forget about everything else?
- Does your involvement in gambling make it hard for you to concentrate on school work or other work?

A PERSONAL STORY OF A RECOVERING GAMBLING ADDICT

Some Are Addicted to Alcohol... I'm Addicted to Gambling

A thick, dark cloud settled over my spirit as I got up to leave. I had spent the last five hours riding a roller-coaster of emotions. I had spent my last dime. I didn't have enough change for bus fare or even a phone call. I had spent every cent I had.

It was a long, long walk to my apartment that night. I had a lot of time to think.

How did I ever get into this state? How could I ever become a gambling addict? I didn't even like to gamble—at first. My mind shifted to rewind as I flashed back to the first time I ever set foot in a bingo parlor.

The first few years of my family life were pretty rough. My father left home when I was about six and he never came back. That's when my mom began drinking. Because of her alcohol addiction she couldn't take care of us. My grandparents took us in. Other alcoholic families really fall apart. Fortunately, we had our grandparents. They took good care of us.

When I was about twelve I got my first baby-sitting job. I made five dollars. Not only did my mom drink, she also loved to go to bingo and took me with her. I lost my hard-earned five dollars. It really upset me. I don't know why I ever went back because I didn't like bingo at all.

By the time I was 14, I was going quite often. Grandpa always took me out on Thursday nights. It was his night out and he needed someone to help watch his cards. He would take either my sister or me with him.

Going to bingo became a habit. I never really had a problem with it until I started earning my own money. When I was 18 I started to get extra money. That's when I really began to have problems with gambling.

There were occasions when I would go out and blow $300 at one time. Then I'd realize what I had done and I'd straighten out. I struggled like this until they opened up the McPhillips Street Station casino in Winnipeg. I remember the first time I walked in there. I hadn't really planned on going but my friend suggested it and I went along. I didn't have any money that first time. We just walked in and saw the place.

When I got money I went back there. I went crazy. From then on it seemed I was always spending my money there.

During my late teen years my income was not regular. So my gambling was rather irregular. But I was spending more and more time at the casino and losing more and more money.

Then something began happening in my family. My cousin and her husband became Christians after watching a television program. Shortly after that they began attending a gospel preaching church in their neighborhood. They were the first Christians in our family. I kept hearing that others in our family were becoming

Christians. I had no idea what it was. One day my cousin stopped by to visit.

"Hi, Mike!" I said as I opened the door.

"Crystal, you're going to hell!" That's how he greeted me. He never said another word but turned and walked away.

Immediately I was convicted in my spirit that what he just told me was true. But he didn't give me any explanation of how not to go to hell. I had this information in the back of my mind for about the next four months.

One day I went to baby-sit for another cousin and her husband. While I was there she explained to me how to become a Christian. By that time I was ready because I'd spent four months trying to figure out how to become a Christian.

My life was pretty messed up. When I was 17 I became pregnant and it wasn't the best relationship with the father. That's when I met Jesus. I prayed and asked Jesus Christ into my life. Since then I've known that the Lord is with me. I talk to Him all the time. I'm always aware that Someone is with me no matter what I'm going through.

Although I was now following Jesus I still couldn't shake the gambling. I'm not so sure I wanted to. I was having a lot of fun. But I was losing a lot of money too.

I don't know what it is about gambling that is so addictive. One time I walked into the McPhillips Street Station when I had about $600 on me. I spent $20 and I won $250. Logically, I should have left. But I continued to gamble and lose until I had only $90 left from the $600. I stayed there until three o'clock in the morning when the Station closed. I just couldn't get up and leave. I should have but I just couldn't.

I don't like losing any money at all when I'm gambling. When I blow the first $20 then I have to get it back. Then it's $40, then $60.

When I'm winning I'm up and I can spend the money. Then it gets to the place where I can never catch up.

When I think of going gambling I feel happy. When I'm there, if I'm winning, I'm happy. If I'm losing, I get very upset. I won't leave unless I start winning or else I'm broke.

During the years when I was gambling and losing the most, I had a friend who thought he was helping me. When I'd blow my money he'd give me some money to buy groceries. He thought he was helping but he wasn't because I never really faced the consequences for a long time.

I really had a good relationship with this person but I learned that he was hurting me more than he was helping. I borrowed money for food and after I gambled away my rent money he would give me money for the rent. It got so bad that I soon owed him over $3000.

It took him a long time to figure out that he wasn't helping me but I guess he was afraid of losing me.

Finally, he told me that he wouldn't help me any more unless I got help. The safety net was gone. I had to face the consequences of my actions. Then I realized I couldn't keep going on like this.

I went for counseling. I wasn't ready. I went for help because it was the condition for getting more money. My mind and heart weren't ready.

It wasn't long before I was back gambling.

I continued to play bingo and the slot machines. The slot machines or VLTs (Video Lottery Terminals) are far more addictive than bingo.

I don't buy lottery tickets. I had a math teacher who told me that the odds of winning the lottery are one in 14 million. The odds don't get any better if you buy more tickets. I thought those odds were too big for me.

Sometimes when I walk into a gambling parlor or casino I say to myself, "I know I'm going to walk out of here broke," but I walk in anyway.

I liken my addiction to an alcoholic. An alcoholic can't stop with one drink. I can't stop with just one game.

The most I've ever won is $1,000. The most I ever lost at one time was $800. That may not seem like a lot of money to some people but I'm on welfare. My whole check for the month is $1,000. That meant I couldn't pay my rent. When I lose money that should have been used for bills I feel really horrible. Sometimes I felt like killing myself. After I walk out of there I think I should have known better. I can't walk into a casino and say I'm going to spend only $20. And I'm not satisfied with winning $20; it has to be at least $100.

After I lost everything, and had to walk home, that's when I realized I needed help, I wanted help.

My friends introduced me to Freedom in Christ

Ministries. I went through their program about a year ago. That has really helped me a lot. I found out that my gambling problem isn't the issue; it's only a symptom of a more serious problem. A lot of it had to do with hurts and abuse from years earlier. I had a lot of anger and bitterness over the way we were treated.

When I was young my mom had a boyfriend and they had kids together. They favored these children, but my siblings and I were given nothing. She just didn't give us stuff and I grew up hating being poor and seeing no way out. I guess gambling gave me a little bit of hope that someday I could win and maybe get some of the stuff I wanted.

I didn't go gambling for nearly four months. That was the first time that I had any victory over it.

I've found that one of the ways to stay away from gambling is to stay in God's Word. I read my Bible every day and I'm memorizing Scripture. I'm trying not to go by my feelings any more. I'm trying to keep things in order in my life. I believe only the Lord can give a person victory over gambling.

Also, I need to be accountable to someone. When you're trying to let go of an addiction, don't lie. Don't deceive people about why you need money. You have to be more open to let people know what's going on.

While I can't say that I've won the war over my gambling addiction, it is so much easier. If you are struggling with gambling I would strongly urge you to get help. I recommend the Freedom in Christ program. Turn to

Jesus and ask Him to heal you of your addiction. It won't be easy but you will find freedom.

Names have been changed or left out to protect the people mentioned.

List of writers and contributors to the topic of GAMBLING:

Anthony T. Evans – taken from "Tony Evans Speaks Out On Gambling and the Lottery" © 1995 by Anthony T. Evans. Moody Press. Used by permission

Gam-Anon International Service Office Inc., New York

FastFacts on Gambling – the Awareness & Information Unit of The Addictions Foundation of Manitoba, 1996

Alberta Alcohol and Drug Abuse Commission – used with permission

R. Gupta, J. Deverensky & M. Edmond - *Factors Underlying Gambling Behavior and Risk-taking in Children and Adolescents.* McGill University. 1994.

Ken C. Winter, Randy Stinchfield, Jayne Fulkerson - Patterns and Characteristics of Adolescent Gambling. Journal of Gambling Studies. Vol. 9(4). Winter 1993.

Robert Ladouceur & Chantal Mireault - Gambling Behaviors Among High School Students in the Quebec Area. *Adolescent Gambling Behaviors.* 1988.

Henry Lesieur; Robert Klein - Pathological Gambling Among High School Students. *Addictive Behaviors.* Vol. 12. 1987. *Taken from Fast Facts on Gambling,* The Awareness & Information Unit of The Addictions Foundation of Manitoba. Used by permission.

Minnesota Council on Compulsive Gambling - Data taken from a survey of Minnesota Public School Students in 1992 and 1995 by Randy Stinchfield, PhD.

CHAPTER FIVE

Does Sexual Brokenness Still Call Your Name?

DEALING WITH AIDS IN THE NATIVE COMMUNITY

1. We have a need to understand our sexuality.

As individuals we all realize that we are sexual beings. We are designed to need and take joy in sexual love. This is God's design. He intended us to have this need and to appreciate sexual love. He taught in Scripture that our sexual being was to be fulfilled, and that joy was to occur within the relationship of a man and a woman entering into a commitment that would last throughout life. This is what God intends for us to anticipate and to enjoy. Unfortunately, we live in a world where God's priorities and God's plan aren't uppermost in people's minds. We live in a society that is saturated with sexual messages. Even though sex is good it can become so bad, evil and destructive to people and families. It can lead to spousal and child abuse.

Unfortunately, even in marriage, sex is often depreciated and thought to be of little value in our marriage relationships. Because of the influence of the media, people believe that the only way to have good sex is outside of marriage.

Sexual love, the physical union that we as human beings have been created by God to enjoy, is something that Christian churches need to teach. We need to instruct this beginning with children in our homes and Sunday Schools. We need to teach people correctly about what God intends.

2. Our churches need to be places that are committed to preventing illness and promoting health and happiness.

We live in a world where we're being told that we can and should enjoy experiences through substance abuse, drug use and that this can be meaningful, even significant. The church should be a place where we can fellowship, have the intensity of experience, and where we can enjoy and appreciate each other. In this way substance abuse and other things that cripple us can be put aside.

We need to be able to be ourselves and be accepted. This should be true of churches throughout our community and our world.

3. People who get infected with the HIV virus become lonely and are often discriminated against.

They often find themselves trying to hide the fact that they're infected with the virus. They're worrying about the illness and how it will affect them. It is a very difficult life.

We are increasingly going to have these people in our communities. We're going to have to learn how not to be afraid of them or fearful of catching the disease. We cannot discriminate against them. We have to recognize that we're all cut out of the same mold. We're all people who, apart from the grace of God working in our lives, would have experienced the same kind of response to temptation. We too may have made decisions that would have led us to take the same kind of risk-taking resulting in infection with the HIV virus.

There's no room for us to feel better than anyone else, or to feel that we are somehow superior to individuals who have been infected with HIV. Within the Body of Christ there's a oneness that accepts and provides support, encouragement, hope and the willingness to walk down this road together.

4. In our world and even in our own community and family there are going to be crises occurring because of this disease.

AIDS already is killing one person in forty each year—very many people know friends, neighbors, and relatives who are ill and dying with AIDS. We want to prevent a sense of hopelessness. We want to offer hope and to let these people know there are answers. We need to stand and say we are no longer going to let people think of a horrible future and the wretchedness of this disease. We are going to say there is hope.

People do need to be encouraged to face the difficulties of life. It isn't easy to be monogamous. It's not easy for many people to have happy, fulfilled sexual lives within the marriage relationship. It isn't always the easiest way to go. It is easy sometimes to reject our faith and to assume that we can find happiness in other kinds of experiences that lead to risky behavior.

We need to be a body of individuals that will help and support each other to make the right decisions that will lead to health, happiness and fulfillment. We need to set examples in our behavior.

We need to organize ourselves to help government make good decisions, to help society to make the kind of decisions to prevent the spread of this disease.

NATIVE COMMUNITIES LAG
IN AIDS EDUCATION

Attending the Eleventh International AIDS Conference were over 15,000 scientists, activists, patients and media representatives from 125 countries around the world. There were over 100 sessions. None of them dealt with Aboriginal AIDS concerns. There were only two Native groups that set up information booths on the floor of the convention center. This only points to how far behind Aboriginal communities are in getting out the message about AIDS.

According to statistics, 513,486 people have been diagnosed with the HIV virus in the United States as of December 1995. Of these, 1,333 were American Indians. In Canada there are an estimated 45,000 Canadians infected with the HIV virus. As of January 1996, 176 AIDS cases were reported among Canada's Aboriginal people representing 1.4 percent of all cases.

A look at the numbers gives a deceiving picture. One might believe that AIDS is spreading at a much slower rate in our Native communities in comparison to the non-Native populations. However, a more accurate picture may indicate just the opposite. In both the United States and Canada, up to 40 percent of reported cases don't include the ethnic background. This means that the correct number of infected Aboriginal people may be much higher.

Many among our own people have long felt that AIDS was "someone else's problem: it won't affect us." The truth is that no group of people will be exempt from

AIDS or the effects of the disease. Health authorities tell us that one out of every five Americans personally know a neighbor, close friend or family member who has AIDS. The numbers aren't much different in Canada.

Health Canada warns that the number of adult female Aboriginal AIDS cases is higher than in the non-Native population. Prostitution, injected drug use, and unprotected sex may be the cause for the higher numbers among Native women. Another Ontario study found that 90 percent of people on the reserves over the age of 15 were sexually active and 41 percent said they had had sex without a condom.

According to AIDS education spokesperson, Barbara Anne McKinnon, this means that the message about AIDS isn't reaching Native people.

> *"A lot of the young people think it's a gay disease, that it's a city thing; it's not going to come to their small town because they're so young... they're so full of life and nothing bad can happen to them."*

HIV-positive people are also more prone to infection from diseases like tuberculosis (TB). The areas with the increasing number of AIDS cases have also seen increases in the number of TB cases. Natives are a high-risk group for contracting TB.

The most important aspect of AIDS education is making sure people know how to avoid HIV. McKinnon says,

> *"We have to provide education and provide ways of prevention in a big way."*

AIDS workers should also be aware of the importance of teaching moral values and abstinence as the ultimate prevention of the spread of the HIV virus.

This book presents the issue in a manner different from what you will read or hear in most of the media. AIDS comes mostly as the result of sin, either through an immoral lifestyle or the result of another person's sin. But many people have or will get infected through no fault of their own. Doctors and nurses are at risk. Police and emergency personnel are at risk. Those who need blood may get the HIV virus and babies born to mothers with HIV are at risk. AIDS in its own ugly way deals many innocent people a deadly blow.

AIDS is one of many problems men and women experience because of mankind's fallen nature and separation from God. Hope for the person involved in sexual sins or with AIDS involves more than just changing our habits or treating the disease. There is a spiritual struggle and a great gap between God and man which must be resolved. True change and lasting hope come only through a new birth into the family of God through faith in Jesus Christ.

We also know that people involved in sinful lifestyles and people with AIDS are our neighbors. We need to reach out with Jesus' love to the homosexual, the adulterer, the prostitute, the drug abuser and the person with AIDS. We can't allow fear, hate and hypocrisy to stand in the way of reaching out. When we understand our own sinfulness before our Creator and have experienced God's grace through His Son, then we will be able to help those who so desperately need our help—both those living in sexual sin and those already receiving the wages for their sins.

AIDS—GOING TO BE AROUND FOR A LONG TIME

An interview with Dr. Allan Ronald, Former Infectious Diseases Consultant at St. Boniface Hospital and Associate Dean—Research at the University of Manitoba, Winnipeg, Manitoba.

When we think of AIDS (Acquired Immune Deficiency Syndrome), HIV (Human Immunodeficiency Virus) and other sex diseases, there are a lot of questions. Most of our fears or confusion come because of unanswered questions. Dr. Ronald has done much AIDS research and worked with patients both in North America and Africa.

IL: *How did the HIV or AIDS virus start?*
Dr. Ronald: We don't know exactly where the virus came from. It's very controversial and creates a lot of unhappiness amongst anyone who is blamed for starting the disease. There is some evidence to say that it began in Zaire, although the first patients that were seen with the disease were in New York and Los Angeles. The virus has been around since at least the mid-1970s. The virus likely

appeared from some primate monkey virus. It began to grow in the human genital track and spread quickly in the late 1970s and early 1980s because of multiple sexual contacts. Lots of people didn't start to die from this virus until the early 1980s.

IL: *If a person gets the HIV virus, how long will it be until he gets sick from AIDS?*

Dr. Ronald: It takes anywhere from four to ten years according to our best information. If 50 people were to get infected today with the HIV virus, the 50th person would get ill ten years from now. The first person would not get sick for four or five years. It's a disease that's like an iceberg because we really don't know the problem until we start testing people to see if they're infected.

IL: *Has a cure been found for AIDS?*

Dr. Ronald: There is no cure for AIDS once someone is infected with the virus. Once a person is infected they will always be infected. Researchers have made significant progress in drug research, which has enhanced the lives of those with HIV and increased their lifespan. But we still do not have a cure for AIDS.

IL: *If there is no cure, what progress have doctors made in treating someone who is HIV positive?*

Dr. Ronald: If a person is infected and in good health, the goal is to keep them healthy for as long as possible. Instead of ten years, if we could make it fifty years before someone who's infected becomes ill, that would be great. It used to be that once a person got ill with AIDS they lived about ten months. That has now changed. Now those who are HIV positive live anywhere from 24 months to ten years.

IL: *How is the AIDS virus spread?*
Dr. Ronald: It became apparent by about 1985 that the disease was spread mainly through homosexual men in the U.S. and throughout the Western countries. In Africa it is spread mainly through heterosexual contact between men and women. There the virus is spread mainly through contact with prostitutes. Men sleep with these women and then return home and spread the disease to their wives.

IL: *What is the best way to stop the spread of AIDS?*
Dr. Ronald: We need to get the message across to everyone that multiple sexual partners is a risk that isn't worth taking. We were not meant to have more than one sexual partner. Getting other diseases (syphilis, gonorrhea, etc.) is not good either. Also we're seeing a lot of Native women who are infertile and unable to have children. This is the horrible result of these other sexual diseases.

The message has to get to people everywhere in the world that starting sex at a very young age opens the door to greater risk of getting AIDS. A girl having sex at 15 with someone who is infected is at much higher risk of getting AIDS than a girl who has sex at 22. At an older age her sexual organs have changed making it much more difficult for her to get infected than at a younger age.

IL: *How can we teach our young people about the dangers of having sex outside of marriage?*

Dr. Ronald: We need to be able to talk with our kids openly in the home about sex. They need to know that sex outside of marriage is not only their problem. It is everybody's problem. God gave us a sex drive that is wonderfully fulfilled in the kind of marriage that He hoped for us to enter. The world is filled with sexual failures, including accounts in the Bible, as well as everyday failures of people who have let their sex drive destroy them. We have to help kids to see that a fellow doesn't need to sleep with his girlfriend in order to be "macho." The macho guy is the one who can control his sex drive and have a healthy relationship with his girlfriend. He's a fellow who can look forward to a happy sexual relationship after he marries. A girl needs to know that she doesn't have to have sex with a boy to prove to him that she loves him.

IL: *So what's the best way to stop AIDS?*

Dr. Ronald: There would be no HIV virus if there were no multiple sex partners. The whole spread of AIDS is because we have multiple partners. If we had one-partner relationships there wouldn't be any spread of HIV.

There is concern in our Native communities about sexual abuse and individuals with multiple sex partners. This concern must not be repressed. We need to talk openly about sexuality and deal with these issues.

IL: *Is there such a thing as "safe sex"?*

Dr. Ronald: We don't use the term "safe sex" anymore. There is no such thing as absolutely "safe sex" but there is "safer sex." People who use condoms reduce the risk by 90 percent or more. Instead of having one bullet in ten in your gun it's one in one hundred. It does reduce the risk. Condoms reduce infection but it's not absolute. Only sex within marriage is safe sex. For people who refuse to change their behavior and continue to practice "high risk" sex, then condoms are safer than nothing at all, but it's not "safe sex."

IL: *Why have we not done more to encourage teens and adults to abstain from having sex outside of marriage?*

Dr. Ronald: Even though the number one wish of human beings in the U.S. and Canada is to have a happy family, that's not how society is currently operating. The number one issue of society is one's personal pleasure. Society pushes for individual rights in order to have all the pleasure they can. Our whole society feeds people sexual pleasure. The average cable TV viewer can see 3,000 couples in bed in a year, and less than ten percent of them are shown as married couples. Society (TV, books and movies) says that you can't enjoy sex if you are married. Even though most people don't behave this way this is what society is pushing.

IL: *Reports tell us that the rate of sexually transmitted diseases (STD) is three times higher for Native people than for North American society in general. What does this mean for the spread of AIDS?*

Dr. Ronald: Having many different sexual partners, including prostitutes, and the fact that Native people have a higher rate of sexual diseases (STDs) are two major concerns. HIV is getting a "toe-hold" in most communities including Native communities. Once it gets a "toe-hold," it will spread more quickly if individuals are having more than one sex partner. This is a major public health concern. Hopefully it is a Native concern too.

IL: *So what's the future for AIDS and for us? How can we change the situation?*

Dr. Ronald: AIDS is a virus that's going to be around for a long time. All of us have to think about how we can prevent it from affecting us as individuals, causing illness or death. Also, we need to know how we can help society deal with the problem.

IL: *What should married couples do?*

Dr. Ronald: As married men and women we need to be committed to our spouses. We need to have happy, loving relationships which include healthy, happy, sexual relationships. That way neither of us have any reason for leaving the relationship. We should model this to our kids, our church and community. If we are doing this we don't need to worry about getting HIV.

IL: *And for young people?*

Dr. Ronald: Consider carefully the consequences of getting sexually-transmitted diseases. I would not put myself at risk of getting any of them, including AIDS, because of what they could do to me, my wife and to my children.

SAFE SEX IS A MYTH
by Dr. Bruce Dunn

The World Health Organization estimates that there are between 30 and 40 million people worldwide who have contracted HIV (Human Immunodeficiency Virus) which causes the disease commonly known as AIDS (Acquired Immune Deficiency Syndrome).

It is becoming clearer each day that we are living in a very impure world. The spread of deadly sexual diseases has led many people to take many steps to insure what they call "safe sex." These are not based on morality but on a fear of disease.

There are about forty sexually transmitted diseases (STDs). The most renowned at the moment is AIDS but there are herpes, syphilis, gonorrhea and a host of others. Some of them are incurable while for others there is hope for recovery. That's the kind of world we're living in.

Directly or indirectly, sexual activity is more encouraged than ever. Television advertising, talk shows, comedies, magazines and movies all make it perfectly proper and smart to "sleep around." It has been a problem since the beginning of time but today the abuse of sex has never been greater.

Safe sex is sex within marriage. The various devices promoted today for safe sex are not safe. Anywhere from 10 to 15 percent of condoms, perhaps even 25 percent according to some sources, are not completely reliable. It's Russian roulette and playing with death when condoms or other devices for safe sex are used. There is no such thing as safe sex except in the area of marriage and faithfulness to a partner.

In all the talk about sex do you notice how little is said about God? He's never mentioned. It's another example of how the Lord is being shut out from our society. People have other gods.

We *must* begin with God. As the Creator He made man after His own image and after His own likeness. In addition to being the Creator He is also the communicating God, talking with us supremely through the Lord Jesus Christ who came as God in the flesh. It says in the first verse of the Gospel of John,

The Word was in the beginning. The Word was God.

Then it says,

Christ became human flesh and lived among us. We saw His shining greatness. This greatness is given only to a much-loved Son from His Father. He was full of loving-favor and truth (John 1:14 NLB).

He has also communicated with us through the written Word: and why not? If He is the only God worthy of the name, perfect in His love for His creation, all-powerful, all-knowing, and present everywhere, should we not expect from Him some reliable communication that will tell us how to live? That just makes good sense. Surely God can be expected to do at least as well toward His creation as good mothers and fathers do toward their children: to give them counsel and guidance for the future, especially regarding eternity. He's a communicating God.

Some of the clearest passages in God's Word about sex sins are found in Leviticus. It's interesting that at least 37 times in Leviticus we find the phrases, "The word of the Lord" or "The Lord spoke unto Moses saying." Those seals of God's authorship not only apply to the passages dealing with priestly service but also to the teachings about proper and improper sex. Leviticus 18 describes lifestyles that would bring divine judgment, every perversion of sex you could imagine: between relatives and friends, in-laws, male and female, heterosexual and homosexual, even bestiality (sex with animals). These warnings all bear the divine stamp, "Thus saith the Lord."

This is the God who stopped after every stage of creation and said, "It is good." That is, until He created man. Then God said,

> *It is not good that the man should be alone. I will make him a helper suitable for him* (Genesis 2:18).

To fill the void God created woman. Jesus said in Matthew 19, *Male and female created He them.*

Not male and male, or female and female. Male and female, in paradise before sin came into the world, in an ideal state at an ideal time. God became the planner and designer of marriage and performed the first wedding ceremony, bringing the man and woman together.

I think it's right to say that, with the exception of personal conversion, marriage is the most important of all earthly events in the life of a man or a woman. God intended it that way.

Hebrews 13:4 says,

Marriage should be respected by everyone.

Some versions rightly translated this verse,

Let marriage be honorable and let the bed be undefiled.

Then it goes on to say,

God will punish those who do sex sins and are not faithful in marriage.

Fornicators dishonor marriage before it takes place. Adulterers dishonor marriage after it takes place. Marriage is honorable.

Marriage is honored by virtue of being the first divine appointment of God. It was made sacred within paradise itself by the Son of God who chose to be born of a woman. The Son of God honored marriage in His parables and spoke often about the marriage feast. Today, marriage is being attacked and slaughtered all over the world.

What is marriage for? First, it's for bringing children into the world. Marriage is also presented to prevent immorality. The apostle Paul wrote,

It is good if a man does not get married. But because of being tempted to sex sins, each man should get married and have his own wife. Each woman should get married and have her own husband. The husband should please his wife as a husband. The wife should please her husband as a

wife (1 Corinthians 7:1-3 NLB).

The reason the husband should please his wife and the wife should please her husband is so that we don't encourage our partner to wander around with someone else.

The Bible is full of examples of people who did not obey God's commandments about sex and the tragic results that followed. It starts in Genesis chapter six with the filth and corruption of the world that brought the judgment of the flood.

We can't forget the story of Sodom and Gomorrah, cities destroyed because of their perversion and violence. Then shortly after their escape from Sodom, Lot's daughters made him drunk, slept with him, and had babies who grew to be some of Israel's greatest enemies. As well there were Samson, Solomon, and Ahab, men who married non-believing women and brought disaster on their people.

One shining positive example is Joseph in the house of Potiphar. Every day Potiphar's wife tried, unsuccessfully, to get him into bed with her. Finally he fled from the house leaving his coat in her hands. She falsely accused Joseph of raping her. Through the entire time of temptation Joseph's attitude was summed up in this statement:

How then could I do this sinful thing, and sin against God? (Genesis 39:9 NLB).

Do you hear young men saying that today? No.

"Let's go to the motel," they say. "Just be sure you have your condoms to make it safe. I know they're only 10, 20, 25 percent safe, but let's take a chance."

Moving to the New Testament, Jesus described the times in which he lived as "a sinful and adulterous generation" (Mark 8:38). Peter speaks of a time when people will have "their eyes full of sex sins. They never have enough sin" (2 Peter 2:14 NLB). Jude warns against sex sins by referring to the people of Sodom and Gomorrah who "were full of sex sins and strong desires for sinful acts of the body" (Jude 7 NLB).

One of the clearest portions of Scripture on the subject of human sexuality and its perversion is Romans chapter one, beginning with verse 21. The downward spiral of sexual sin begins with a rejection of God.

> *They did know God, but they did not honor Him as God. They were not thankful to Him and thought only of foolish things. Their foolish minds became dark. They said that they were wise, but they showed how foolish they were. They gave honor to false gods that looked like people who can die and to birds and animals and snakes. This honor belongs to God Who can never die* (Romans 1:21-21 NLB).

Instead of looking upward and outward to God, mankind began to look downward and inward to man. The result was idolatry, worshipping both men and beasts. Man prefers to look to himself rather than to God. You don't hear many people talk about God anymore; man has become central. What happens when mankind worships itself? God says:

God let them follow their sinful desires which lead to shame. Women used their bodies in ways God had not planned. In the same way, men left the right use of women's bodies. They did sex sins with other men. They received for themselves the punishment that was coming to them for their sin (Romans 1:26-27).

When you worship the creature instead of the Creator, your entire life, including your physical desires, is thrown out of its proper channel. You break down the barriers of sex and destroy the three-way relationship God has ordained between a husband, his wife, and the Lord. In the end you will reap in your own body the rotten fruit of that sin and will be drowned by sex sins.

If you have been guilty of sexual sin in the past I must add a word of consolation. God forgives and cleanses in the name of Jesus. By the Spirit of God you can get a new life if you turn to the Lord, confess your sin and place your faith completely in Him.

WORDS OF ENCOURAGEMENT

by Michael Johnston

If you have the HIV virus or are ill with AIDS you may be looking for some miraculous cure. It's important to know that the only hope that will never let you down is found in God our Creator. The only way to find the peace He offers is through a relationship with His Son, Jesus Christ.

The only way to prove that God is real and keeps His promises is to take a step of faith. It isn't easy to do. For many it will be like stepping off a cliff blindfolded. I can tell you from my own experience that God will catch you going off that cliff. He is truly faithful to His Word. He will be there for you.

If you are struggling with homosexual desires I know the struggle and pain is real. It is not something you have imagined: I've been there.

God understands our pain. He understands what we don't understand. He understands our struggle.

The reason we are in this position and have these basic desires is because we are separated from the very God who made us. We are separated from His perfect love and acceptance. We can look for substitutes in many places. We can look for it in sex, in alcohol, in our jobs or even in religion.

There is only one place that we are ever going to find real love. That is in Jesus Christ.

Won't you give your burdens to the Lord and let Him take over?

My Search for Love
by Michael Johnston

The lights were flashing. The music was loud and vibrant. A disco beat. A lot of people were talking and dancing and having a good time. I had never been in that kind of place before. I was under age at the time so just the idea of being there was great. It was the party scene and that's what I wanted to be a part of.

I was there with a friend from high school. He had invited me to go with him to this night club. It was a gay bar. This place was very exciting! It was just the kind of thing that puts you into a mood of letting loose, setting aside your morals.

As we left the bar that night my friend invited me to spend the night. I accepted. That night I had my first sexual experience, a homosexual one. This wasn't the first time I had dealt with the issue of sex. It wouldn't be the last either.

I grew up pretty much like most boys. However, my dad was in the U.S. military and we traveled around quite a bit. When he went to Vietnam we moved closer to my grandparents, uncles and aunts. They were living in Texas at the time.

After moving to Texas we began attending a local Christian church. There I heard a message that was new to me. I heard about salvation for the first time. They were saying that I needed a Savior to cleanse me of my sins.

Shortly after we started going to this church my sister turned her life over to Jesus Christ. After that God's Spirit started speaking to me. I recognized that there was something wrong in my life.

I was ten years old at the time. I didn't know much about God but I did understand that there was a place called heaven and a place called hell. I knew that if you had to choose, one was better than the other. The only way to go to heaven was to be saved through Christ. I did understand that being saved was something I could not do for myself. It was something that God had to do for me.

I used to sneak up into a little tower in the church. While on my knees, I'd cry out to God, "Please God, save me! I don't want to go to hell!"

Not long after that at an evening service I was overcome with a strong feeling that God had done something in my life. I went forward and accepted Christ as my Savior. Two or three weeks later I was baptized.

That year our family was in a lot of turmoil. Mom missed Dad a lot. I didn't know when Dad was going to come home or even if he would for sure. It was a tough year for me because for the first time I was among kids who really had nothing in common with me. I guess this was kind of my taste of the real world. I didn't enjoy it and pretty much kept to myself.

The year that my father came back home the military moved us to Alaska. Going to Alaska was exciting, especially for a boy my age.

My mom started to work and I tried to fit into a new school. It was during this time that I was introduced to pornography.

On the school bus one day, the guys were passing around a book of nude pictures. This was the first time in my life that I had ever really thought about sex. Probably if I hadn't seen this stuff I would not have thought about sex for a couple more years. It began to be a real problem for me.

On other occasions sex magazines were passed among the fellows. My introduction to sex told me it was something that was dirty, something you shouldn't do, but something that all the guys seemed to want. It became a goal for me. I thought, "If I have sex that will make me somebody that's important."

During junior and senior high school I became involved more heavily with pornography and masturbation. I was also introduced to alcohol and marijuana. It wasn't long before I became addicted to the pleasures that sex and drugs provided. I could enjoy these things in private without having to talk to or be around other people. I didn't share it with anyone.

At the same time I was beginning to face peer pressure. I felt a need to belong, to be accepted and approved by other kids my age. Because I was pretty much a loner all these years I really hadn't learned how to talk to people and make friends easily. Doing drugs and being around others who did drugs gave me a sense of being accepted.

From marijuana I went on to stronger drugs like acid. I started high school as what appeared to be an average student who loved to party. I really enjoyed having good times and I was able to stay out of trouble. It wasn't because I wasn't doing things that would get me into trouble. It's just that I was good at not getting caught.

Nothing really happened during this time that would have made me stop and question the direction I was taking. As long as I was having fun I thought there was no reason to question what was going on. After all, others were doing it too!

In my junior year my family moved to Virginia. While there I continued my involvement with drinking and taking drugs. I still had a strong desire to become sexually active. I felt this was something that would make me the man I should be, more acceptable in the eyes of other fellows. Up to this point I hadn't yet had sex with anyone.

My drugs and drinking caused some problems between my parents and me. Many times I would come home stoned. Often I'd stay out drinking all night. I became very rebellious. I decided to leave home.

I'll never forget that day. My mother found the note I left in my bedroom. She came down to the bus station before my bus pulled out and tried to convince me to come back home. My father told me that I was making a mistake but he also wanted me to know that if I left there would always be a place for me at home. (I really didn't understand the importance of that until many years later.)

My mother handed me some money as I got on the bus. I'll never forget watching her as the bus pulled out. She stood by the pole crying. That was a very difficult day. It was hard to see her cry like that. But to be honest, I got five miles down the road and all that was forgotten. I was excited about taking on the world.

That trip took me back to Alaska where I finished my last year of high school. During that year I worked nights and went to school full-time. It was very difficult and tiring. I continued my drug habits and partying, barely making the grades to graduate.

During that year I became close to a fellow I had known since my second year of high school. He was a good dancer and someone I felt really had it all together. He was sexually active and that was important to me. He's the one who took me to that gay bar. That's when I had my first homosexual experience. It wasn't really the actual sex that I enjoyed. What seemed important was that I had finally reached this goal of having sex. That night was also important because this fellow accepted me. He wanted to be very close to me. This just fed on the desire in all of us to have someone accept us. I was lonely with no real friends. I wanted someone to love me.

We all want someone to love us: we look for that in people.

The tragic fact is that we can never really find the love and acceptance we are looking for in other people. A relationship with God is the only place we will ever find that. I didn't learn that until many years and much suffering later.

The years went by and I became involved in many relationships. I ended up going back to Virginia to attend college. It was at this point that my parents found out about my involvement with homosexuality. They were very upset and made it clear that they could not accept it. My father took me to see a military psychologist who told him we just needed to learn to talk to each other. So much for psychiatry!

Also, while in Virginia, I met a fellow and we began a relationship together. This was the first serious relationship I had since entering into the homosexual lifestyle. It was exciting. I had all kinds of ideas and hopes about what it would be like. I guess I thought it was going to be perfect. We saw each other for about a year before we moved in together in Richmond. All relationships have a "honeymoon" period and then you get down to the work of building a relationship. Of course, the problem with a homosexual relationship is that it was never meant to be; you will always have problems that you will not be able to overcome.

Our relationship began to fall apart. The sexual part was getting boring for me. All the sex experiences up to this point had been short-term. I had enjoyed the excitement of finding someone new. There was a thrill in going to the bars and picking someone up, having sex with them for the night and then the next weekend going with someone else. That's what I was used to. So it was difficult staying with one person for a long time.

One day I was flipping across the radio dial. There was a station in Richmond that played gospel music. As I listened to this music the Lord reached out and began to convict me. Deep down I knew that the homosexual lifestyle was wrong. God showed me the Scripture verse (Leviticus 18:22) that says very clearly that a man having sex with another man is sin. It is unacceptable to God. I began to question the commitment I had made to Christ when I was ten years old.

"What did that really mean?" I asked myself. "If living the life of a homosexual is really against God's will, then what does that say about my commitment to Christ?" I felt uncomfortable. I walked away from that homosexual relationship. I shared this with my parents. Needless to say they were very happy.

Shortly after that I moved to Washington, D.C. I had never been in a big city before. Washington has the fourth largest homosexual population in the U.S. I didn't know that at the time.

Determined that the homosexual lifestyle was going to become part of my past, I moved into an apartment just down the street from Dupont Circle. In the Dupont Circle area, there were about three or four gay bars. The Circle is a very popular hangout for gays, especially during the summer. I didn't know that when I moved there.

I continued to smoke my marijuana. My only relationship with God was spending a few minutes reading a devotional guide called *Daily Word*. I didn't even do that every day. I didn't go to church or seek out other Christians. That devotional reading was my only spiritual relationship.

Just being in this city was exciting. I found an exciting job.

Three months went by. I couldn't understand why God hadn't taken this desire away from me. I continued smoking my drugs and lusting.

"God, You're just not doing anything here. I don't understand," I pleaded. "What's the problem?"

Deep down I knew the answer.

I continued to deal with those desires. It got so frustrating I just gave up.

I went back to the bars again. Here I was faced with a whole new exciting world. It was fun, pleasurable and exciting. "After all," I thought to myself, "isn't this what life is all about? Having fun and being happy." This way of thinking was what I was living by. I was tired of fighting and just decided to give in to my desires. I fitted right into the bar scene.

I met a bartender at one of the bars. He was a very popular fellow. It seemed he was everyone's friend. He started buying me drinks and showing me around town. We ended up moving in together and developing a long-term relationship. This turned out to be the longest relationship I would have.

Cocaine was very easy to come by and we did a lot of it along with marijuana and alcohol. I was having the time of my life. There was the excitement and the feeling of being accepted and important. This is what really seemed to cement our relationship.

A year later I talked my partner into going to Alaska to open a gay nightclub. We moved to Anchorage with big plans but they didn't work. When we got there a big battle was going on about liquor licenses and we couldn't seem to get enough money together —a lot of good ideas but no money.

My partner got a job in a new restaurant and I continued working with the government. We built a home out in a small town. Things seemed to be going well. We began building relationships with other homosexual couples. I wasn't willing to walk away from the relationship or the lifestyle. Our partnership was providing the security and love, or at least I thought it was love, that I had longed for and I just wasn't willing to walk away. In the back of my mind I thought that someday I was going to have to stop. I believed that if I was a practicing homosexual when I died I wouldn't go to heaven.

"Sometime before I die," I said to myself, "I've got to walk away from this lifestyle but not right now. I'm having too much fun."

After about three years things began to fall apart. My partner became stressed out with his job and moved into the city. Bills began piling up. He finally walked away from his job and left me holding the bag.

I learned very quickly that our relationship, at least for me, was based on financial security. When our future was threatened the relationship got old real fast. Sex became a real bore. I was already seeking sex elsewhere. My partner didn't know it because I kept it hidden from him. During this period I hit the lowest level of my immorality. I was having a lot of one-night stands. I was going to adult bookstores and video places.

Probably six or seven months after this I began to wake up in the middle of the night soaking wet with sweat but I never connected it with AIDS until I went to see my doctor.

On my birthday, March 23, the test's results came back. I was HIV positive—what a birthday present! Stunned, I walked out of the doctor's office very numb all over.

My partner noticed that I was not responsive. He tried to reach out to save our relationship but I didn't want to tell him that I had the virus. Our relationship broke down at that point.

Things got so bad I ended up walking away from the house. For several months I was in a state of shock, not really knowing how to handle things. I just simply stopped paying the bills. Before long I had to declare bankruptcy.

During all of this my mind was kind of dead. I just concentrated on my job and trying to have a good time. I continued having sex with guys. I didn't even tell them I was HIV positive. Not caring for anyone but myself I was spreading the virus around.

During all of these dark days God was there trying to get my attention. He kept convicting me of my sin.

Finally, I decided that I had to walk away from all of this. There was no other choice. If it was going to happen it was going to happen now. I didn't have anything to lose.

Shortly after this I was placed on a special assignment at work. I started working with a woman who was a Christian. She liked to listen to Christian radio. We began listening together. During one of the programs there was an announcement for a Christian concert to be held at a local church. I had heard this singer and really liked his music. "I want to go hear him," I said to myself.

I went. It was scary, not an easy thing for me to do. I walked into that church feeling like I had "homo" stamped all over my forehead. I just felt that when I walked through the door everyone was going to know. Once inside I sat near the middle of the church. The people seemed friendly but I still felt like an outsider.

About halfway through the concert the singer sang the song *Jesus, Lord to Me.* As he sang, the Lord reached out and touched me. I haven't felt that way since the day I was saved. He put His arms around me and said, "Michael, you're my son and I love you. I'm here for you. Come home."

I went back to the church the next Sunday. After the service I went up to the pastor. My legs were shaking.

"Pastor," I said as I grabbed his hand, "two weeks ago I decided to leave the homosexual lifestyle. I need help." He spoke to me just briefly.

"Michael, you need to get into counseling." He called the counseling director and we set up an appointment. Every two weeks for the next six months I met with him. The interesting thing about our times together is that after I shared my story we didn't talk about my homosexual lifestyle. I discovered that homosexuality wasn't my problem. It was just a result of my sin. My disobedience against God was the problem. I realized that I had never understood who I was in Christ and what my relationship to Him was all about.

We spent the next six months working on my walk with Christ. There were several issues I had to deal with. There was the issue of walking away from my homosexual friends, cutting off my relationships. That was very difficult. Every friend I had was homosexual. Being so dependent on other people for acceptance and to suddenly not have any friends was a very scary thing.

God was faithful and provided godly friends and relationships. Now my friendships are with people whose goal is also to seek the Lord in everything they do.

I had to deal with my pride. I'm finding that root problems are not based in relationships with other people. They are based in not understanding my relationship with God and in not trusting and obeying Him regardless of my circumstances and feelings.

We're all born with a broken relationship. We're all seeking love, affirmation and security. God never intended us to find that in other human beings. He always intended that we find it in Him.

For me, AIDS is really a non-issue. It isn't the driving force in my life. Quite honestly, AIDS is the best thing that ever happened to me. Apart from Christ's death on the cross, allowing me to catch the AIDS virus is the single most loving thing my Father could have done for me. He knew what it would take to turn me back to Him. Now I know what it means to have a real relationship with Christ. I've found that knowing God through Jesus Christ is what life is all about.

Names of people or places have been left out or changed to protect those mentioned in this story.

The Missing Bond
by Kenn

It was all set. We had planned it well. My cousin Tommy and I were set to steal some porno magazines from the corner bookstore.

On Saturdays Tommy and I took in a movie at the local movie theater. Next door was the bookstore. When we were in junior high school, porno magazines were displayed on the front counter where anyone could pick them up and take a peek. We decided to each steal a copy. We agreed that Tommy would pick up one porno magazine and I would take another.

Grabbing our copies, we hurried out and ran down the alley. When we stopped to look at our stolen prizes I realized I'd picked up the wrong magazine. I opened the magazine to find pictures of naked men.

I had never seen any magazines showing nudity

before. Sex was never talked about in my family. I was shocked but found myself almost immediately aroused.

I threw away my magazine but Tommy kept his. Later that evening I went back to the dumpsite and grabbed the magazine and snuck it home.

Whenever I would look at these pictures, thoughts from my early childhood began pouring back into my mind. Although I come from a Navajo family we weren't brought up in the traditional Navajo way. My father was a minister in New Mexico. I am the youngest of six children.

Stealing that first magazine started a habit which I kept up for many years. I would take them from different stores all across town. I would look at the pictures and get excited.

My home life was very strict. There was this feeling that we had to be the "perfect family." My dad was popular on the reservation. People respected his preaching and pastoral work. I was brought up to fear God. We were taught that anything done against God would be punished. This was very hard for me to accept.

My dad would not allow us to have friends who were not from the same church as we were. As a child I didn't understand why I couldn't have friends from other churches. My dad was very busy with his church work, preaching all over the Navajo reservation. He really didn't have time for the family.

As a little boy my first friends were little neighborhood girls. We played Barbie dolls together. Dressing up and playing with these girls was a big secret. Somehow I knew it wasn't right for me as a boy to be playing with dolls. A few times I was caught by my sister or brothers. They scolded me and gave me a hard time about it. This had a powerful effect on me.

For most of my childhood I grew up pretty much alone. From the time I was five my three oldest brothers and sister were off at a boarding school. For several years I only saw them on weekends. There was no bonding with my family members.

About the time I started junior high I began to feel that my interests were more towards fellows than girls. I began to think I was abnormal.

Junior high was also the time I began taking gym classes and participate in the initiation of undressing and showering with my classmates. I wasn't aroused by the boys, but the gym teachers who would come in with their shirts off turned me on. I used to admire their bodies and fantasize about them.

All this time I knew deep down inside that this was wrong. It was a big secret. I was scared to death to think of what would happen if anyone found out about my magazines or the thoughts that flowed through my mind.

During my junior high summers we had a group of Christian college-age fellows come to our church to help with our children's summer activities. They were young and white. I wanted to talk to them but didn't know how. I wanted to have some male friends but I didn't know how to get a friendship off the ground. I thought if I could get to know a fellow then maybe, just maybe, there was a chance of getting an "arm around the shoulder," a hug or a friendly slap-on-the-back. Just a sign of encouragement and approval. I longed for that. My dad never gave me that and my brothers didn't either.

There was no male bonding at all. The only bonding I had was with my mother. We had a close mother-son relationship. If it wasn't for my mom I don't know where I'd be today. When we were alone in the house together my mom and I would talk. But the way she viewed her Christian faith was very different from the way I saw my faith. My mom's way to deal with problems was to pray about them. That's what these college fellows also told me.

High school was one big blur for me. I had no idea what I wanted to do with my life. My older brother joined the Future Farmers of America (FFA) so I did too. I took a lot of classes I didn't want to take; these were the ones FFA students took. I didn't know what my interests were. No one ever encouraged me to get into art or things that I liked to do.

I had a couple of girlfriends but our relationships were really low-key: no sex. I felt comfortable talking to them but I still had this interest in looking at men. I was still hooked on those magazines.

I was on the high school track team for a short while but it became too competitive for me. There was always pressure to win; we had to win. It just didn't seem right. I just wanted to run for fun. We weren't encouraged to have fun—just run to win. After a while I couldn't take it anymore and dropped out. I continued to run outside of school for my own enjoyment.

I was introduced to alcohol during my junior year in high school. It was something that wasn't allowed in our house. My father hated anything that had to do with alcohol. Many times our doorbell would ring in the middle of the night and my dad would open the door to find drunks on the doorstep. He made it very clear that he wanted me to have nothing to do with alcohol. "Drunks are sinners" was the message I got from him.

My senior year I went to my first party. I got drunk. My classmates, the ones I thought were my friends, made fun of me. They were the popular ones—student council president, cheerleaders and jocks. Even though they all drank they made fun of me because I got drunk the first time I tried alcohol. My embarrassment kept me from drinking for a while after that.

After graduation I took the year off to get a job, a car and save money for college later on.

When I started studies at the University of New Mexico in Albuquerque, I began drinking again. At the same time my parents were going through a lot of disagreements. There were problems in the church and it was creating trouble at home. I didn't like the way my dad was treating my mom. During this time my brothers were all getting married. I didn't even have a girlfriend. This put a lot of stress on me and I began drinking heavily.

It seemed that all I could do at the university was drink. I got involved with a guy sexually but I kept it secret. I really didn't know how to develop friendships. I was lost and my grades showed that I didn't know what I was doing.

My major was architecture. There were things about it that I liked; there were things I didn't like. I quit the university, started at a technical school and ended up getting a job with an architect.

I went to church during my first two years in Albuquerque. During that time I committed myself to Christ but it was all a big lie. I later stopped going.

I had friends but I didn't know how to deal with them. The only thing I knew that would work was alcohol. Alcohol attracted people to me. When I made money I blew it all on alcohol. I drank so much that I started having blackouts. I ran into another car during a blackout and received my first DWI (driving while intoxicated) penalty. That didn't stop me. While working for the architect I received my second DWI.

At the office there was this fellow who kept telling me that I ought to check out a certain church in town. I had a funny feeling that I shouldn't go but I finally did.

The first Sunday the pastor's sermon was meant for me. I felt really at home in this place. The next Sunday a need was announced for counselors for the children's camp. Although I had my doubts as to whether or not I could do this I signed up to be a counselor.

Being involved with these kids was the best weekend of my life. The speaker spoke on prayer. It had a real impact on my life. During the weekend the speaker took me aside and we had a private talk. I opened and shared with him. I told him that I didn't know who I was, that I wanted to know Christ in a personal way. I was crying. We prayed together. That night I turned my life over to Jesus.

Shortly after the kids' camp I was asked to become a Sunday School teacher. I dedicated my life to Christ during this time and was later baptized. I joined the choir and became very active in the church life.

Now that I was a Christian I knew that God wipes away all sin. During my first few years as a Christian my homosexual tendencies were not there. To my shock they came back. I felt terrible.

"What's wrong with me?" I thought to myself. "I'm a Christian, why is this happening?" I didn't know who I could talk to. I thought, "Alcoholism, that's something people will accept. I've been to Alcoholics Anonymous and I've been sober for a couple of years. But homosexuality, that's something people don't talk about." I was really struggling with these thoughts.

During this period I discovered that there were adult bookstores where I could see men having sex with other men. That's where I started going. On my car's bumper I had a little fish symbol, the sign of a Christian. Every time I would go to these bookstores I would back the car in so the fish symbol would be against the wall or fence. Doing this was really bothering me.

Popular Christian singer Steve Green came to Albuquerque for a concert. He has been a favorite of mine. This concert was more than just a musical event. It was a ministry. He said that God loves the alcoholic. I said to myself, "Yeah, I know that." Then he said, "And God loves the homosexual."

"No He doesn't," I thought. At that moment, I just seemed to shut down emotionally.

That night I couldn't sleep. Those words, "God loves the homosexual," were branded in my mind. I got up and started writing Steve Green a letter. I was crying. I told him exactly how I was feeling:

"I really enjoyed your concert but something that really bothered me is what you said about the homosexual. I don't believe that God loves the homosexual." I told him about my alcoholism and about my being in AA. "I need to find some comfort but I just don't know what to do." I explained that this isn't a topic that you can open up and share with just anyone.

Two weeks later a package came for me. Inside was the book *How Can I Tell My Mother?* by Jerry Arterburn (Oliver/Nelson Books). I read right through it. "This is it," I thought to myself. "I'm going to be healed."

Near the end of the book Jerry writes that the practicing homosexual needs counseling. He includes some addresses of places to contact. One of the addresses is that of Exodus International, a Christian ministry to homosexuals wishing to leave the lifestyle. I called them and they sent me a brochure including a list of counseling centers in Canada and the U.S. There were no counseling places listed for New Mexico. There was one in Texas but I didn't want to go there. I finally found a place in Denver, Colorado called Where Grace Abounds. I called them.

"Hi, I'm Kenn and I'm calling from New Mexico," I said. Feeling hesitant to ask for help I felt more comfortable when a fellow by the name of Steve shared a little about himself and the WGA ministry. I thought, "Wow, this is neat. I've found a place where I can talk to people who understand. I won't be shunned." Steve and I started writing letters back and forth. He invited me to come to Denver during my spring break but I backed down and went to California instead. In one of Steve's letters he asked me why I didn't come up to Denver. I remember his ending the letter with "Yours in Christ." I thought to myself, "Man this guy really cares for me."

I decided to go to Denver after school was out in 1989.

My first meeting was a very nervous one. I didn't know anyone or what to expect.

One thing I learned during my ten days in Denver was that I needed to open up to people. I went back home and told two good friends of mine, one male and one female, that I was gay. I opened up to them and lost their friendships!

"Well, this doesn't work," I told myself. I was very down about that but I continued to tell others.

I told my brother. I felt I needed to since he was the one who gave me money to make the trip to Denver in the first place. He listened and accepted what I said.

The next time I was home I told my parents that I would like to talk to them. My dad, being who he is, had stuff to do and wasn't there so I talked to my mom. We both cried. She told me this was an issue we were not going to share with other family members. I respected that. I asked her, "Mom, will you please tell Dad for me?"

Later, she told my dad in Navajo. When I was home the next time I asked Dad if Mom had talked to him. He said, "Yeah, she did. I understand that you are struggling with being gay."

"Yes," I said. He gave me the support Mom had given me. He said he would not talk about it with any-one else.

As things worked out I ended up moving to Denver in order to get counseling from Where Grace Abounds. I started attending the University of Colorado at Boulder. I had a hard time adjusting to life in Colorado but I began to make friends and take inventory of myself.

I got to know a male friend from AA who is a very good friend today. He is the first one I told that I was a homosexual. Also I told my AA sponsor. It was very hard. In order to know myself, I've got to be honest. I needed people and I needed friends. I also needed to get to know who I am.

I started with just a few people in Boulder. What I found is that I was finally able to open up.

April 11th is my AA birthday. This year I celebrated five years of being sober. I wanted to have a party to cel-ebrate this anniversary. I made invitations and invited many friends. Forty people came to my party. It was the most exciting thing ever. I put both my AA and WGA friends together. That was an awesome feeling!

I thank God for the positive changes that have occurred in my behavior and feelings in the past year. I do get lonely but at those times I remember that God has been with me from the first step of my journey and that He will continue to carry me through to the end.

I know I'm not the only Navajo or Native American struggling with homosexuality. I know that by exposing myself God may use it to let others know that they're not alone in their struggle, that He really loves them and that He provides a way out of sexual sin. If those things happen for even one other person then telling my story has been worth it!

List of writers and contributors to the topic of AIDS:
Dr. Allan Ronald, Retired AIDS researcher, Winnipeg, MB
Dr. Bruce Dunn, Late speaker on the Grace Worship Hour, Peoria, Illinois
Michael Johnston – Kerusso Ministries, Virginia Beach, Virginia

CHAPTER SIX

Does the Lure of Pornography Still Call Your Name?

THE POWER OF THE PICTURE
by Jerry Kirk

Pornography in sex magazines, books and on film are not what they used to be. What is called "hard-core pornography" is much more than the pictures that were once found in men's magazines.

What is found in magazines, in X-rated movies and videos and what can be seen on cable television and satellite is violent, dangerous stuff. These pictures no longer just show ladies' beautiful bodies; they show pictures of people having sex with animals, people hurting women and children in violent sex acts. They show people killing other people while doing sex sins.

We want to try to answer three important questions:

Does it hurt those who see it? Can it be habit-forming? What is it doing to our Native society?

When we look around our cities across this continent we see many places where dirty sex magazines are sold. In some states and provinces the laws do not allow stores to put this out where people can look at them. Many stores carry these magazines and books behind the counter. Other states don't have laws to control this so you can find these kinds of magazines right in your corner grocery store.

Not only do stores sell dirty magazines, there are also stores that sell movies that you can take home and watch on your TV set. Other people can watch dirty movies on cable television or by way of satellite that can come from very far away.

Even on our reservations, many of which are far from the cities, we can find dirty magazines, books, videos and TV programs. They are as easy to get as a six-pack of beer. And many of our families have these things right in their homes for their little children to see and hear.

Do dirty pictures hurt those who look at them? Dr. Victor Cline, a doctor at the University of Utah in Salt Lake City says "Yes." He has taken care of hundreds of people with sex problems. Most of these have seen a lot of porno pictures and movies. He has found that there is almost always a four-step path that leads these people down a path full of problems.

First, there is the habit-forming part. A person gets "hooked" on dirty pictures. It is just like getting hooked on cigarettes or alcohol. Sometimes it is more powerful. These pictures give the person a feeling of power and excitement. He keeps coming back for more. He is never satisfied.

Second, there is the need for more shocking and exciting pictures and stories. He asks his wife or girlfriend to do sex sins with him—the same ones he sees in the pictures. Sometimes he forces her. When she turns him down he leaves her. He goes after someone who will give him what he wants.

Third, after a while, the person is no longer bothered by what he looks at. He doesn't think it is wrong to look at those pictures. What was first dirty, sinful, and wrong for him soon becomes good to him. The person begins to believe that everyone looks at those pictures and does those things.

Fourth, the person starts to "act out" or do the things he sees in those magazines and on those videos. What was first like a dream is turned into the real thing.

Pornography: a chain that's hard to break

At the University of California in Irvine, Dr. James L. McGaugh has done studies that show that memories of things people do when they are excited sexually are difficult to erase. This means that things they do when they're thinking dirty thoughts are hard to put out of their minds. It's like the thoughts are glued to the back of their brains.

Dr. McGaugh's studies also show that memories of sex sins get locked in the brain by a special fluid. This fluid makes these thoughts hard to forget. Powerful sex thoughts keep coming back and these make the person do other sex sins.

Police studies have shown that people who look at dirty sex pictures in magazines and in movies do what they see: they act out what their eyes have seen. The Michigan State Police found that in 38,000 cases of sex attacks they have in their files, 41 percent used dirty pictures and/or videos just before or during the time the person did the attack. In a 1958 FBI study which talked with men in prison who had killed a number of people, 81 percent of those killers said they were most interested in dirty sex magazines. They said that's what stirred up their interest in sex.

Pornography is killing our children

There is very little question that men who read sex magazines and watch sex videos attack and abuse women more than men who don't. But there is something much more harmful, something people don't think much about. When parents keep sex magazines in their homes it is likely that their children will find these and look at them. Think about this:

A boy found a copy of a porn magazine and read one of the articles. He was interested so he decided to do what the magazine talked about. He followed the directions and wound up dead. The magazine was lying at his feet when his mother found his cold body.

Two brothers, ages 9 and 10, found some of their parents' sex videos and secretly watched them. They did this for several months, while their mom and dad were at work. They later forced their younger sisters to watch the videos, and do the things they saw, against their will. The boys told them they would shoot them with a BB gun if they told their parents. They kept on doing these terrible things for several years.

In 1986 a witness for an important study, done by the office of the U.S. government's top lawyer, told the following story: "My dad had sex with me when I was eight. He would tell me that it was OK. He would find magazines with articles or pictures that would show father and daughter, mother and son or brother and sister, having sex together. He would say that if it was put in magazines, it had to be all right because magazines could not tell lies."

Pornography is hurting our people

Almost every day we read and hear reports of abuse among our people. A 1986 report in London, Ontario, reported that 71 percent of Native people living in the city had lived with family violence. In a 1985 study of Mi'kmaq women in Nova Scotia, it was shown that 70 percent had been abused by their husbands.

Growing up on the Mississauga reservation in Blind River, Ontario, an Ojibwe teacher said she was "terrorized" by an older brother. She says she still wakes up scared to death after nightmares about her brother.

Sex magazines and movies are coming into our homes in the cities and even on remote reservations.

They're found in our prisons, tempting men and women to do "sex sins" both in the prison and after they get out.

Some people will try to say that the studies about what these magazines and movies do to people are not true. But one thing we know: we don't need to work on a study to know that sex pictures harm our people. We know they harm our women, our children and especially our men.

At the present time almost every community in the U.S. and Canada has laws controlling these kinds of pictures. There needs to be control. The laws need to be enforced and respected or else they should be taken off the books.

As Dr. Cline said, "In a sense our 'drinking water' is poisoned; it is making a lot of people sick. But very few people are doing or saying anything about it. Our people and our country are too precious not to know."

Off a Deep and Dangerous End

by Mike Yorkey and Dean Merrill

Ever wonder where killers get their ideas to abuse, rape and destroy? Often, the answer lies as close as the corner store.

Imagine that you're a scientist working for a large company that makes medicines. One day, after months of hard work, you discover a drug that is a dangerous poison. You find that you can make it very cheaply. How could you be sure this new poison really worked? After all, as a scientist, you're aware how people doubted the University of Utah scientists who told the public about their discovery of "cold fusion."

Would you invite a half-dozen friends over to watch a World Series game and spike their Pepsi to see what happened? Probably not. It would probably be better to kill a few rats used for testing in order to prove your point.

When it comes to mental poison such as "dirty sex pictures and dirty talk," they don't seem to affect rats: it seems to affect only humans. Looking at dirty and violent pictures with brutal rape and sexual torture is like putting gasoline on the fire of a whole lot of murders, rapes and abuse across our countries.

Unfortunately, a scientist's "proof" of the link between dirty sex pictures and crime just isn't there. Who would give people a bunch of sex magazines to read and then sit back to see what kind of terrible acts they would do?

To see the terrible things dirty sex pictures make people do we only have to read our local newspaper. At the beginning of the 1990s we could no longer say that dirty sex pictures are just looking at something bad, a bit of misbehaving. The fact is that dirty sex pictures are a scary business: it's dangerous and it can kill.

When Ted Bundy told the world that pornography led to his cruel killing of young women and children, the nation's newspapers and television just laughed and turned "thumbs down." Yet Bundy was not the first killer to tell of how dirty sex magazines and movies changed the way he thought about women:

In 1987, Richard Brimage of Kingsville, Texas, got Mary Beth Kunkel, 19, to come to his home. "I really wanted to have sex with her and when she did not do so, I killed her," he told police. Brimage choked Kunkel to death then tied her up in the same way that he saw women tied up in a video he had in his living room.

Richard Daniel Starrett of Martinez, S.C. confessed to kidnapping and killing a 15-year-old girl. He is also charged with the sex killings of other young girls. Starrett, who blamed dirty sex pictures for the way he acted, kept a huge pile of dirty magazines in a mini-storeroom he rented. During one raid, police found 935 hardcover and paper back books with pictures of naked men and women, scary pictures that showed people doing angry sex crimes to other people.

When John Weber, 25, of Wausau, Wisconsin was arrested in 1988, police found more than 100 "dirty sex magazines" in his car. Weber, who used to get a thrill when he read these magazines, said that he started this when he was a child. He was found guilty last March of the painful killing of his sister-in-law.

Officials in San Diego believe that Richard Sanders murdered four people, including two children, while making what is called "snuff films" (movies showing real-life killings). He was killed in a gun battle. Sanders was also connected with the sex killings of 40 prostitutes, drug addicts and homeless people.

Two or three times a week Ramon Salcido of Sonoma County, California went to his local video store and rented XXX-rated movies. In April of 1988, Salcido went crazy, killing his wife, mother-in-law, two sisters-in-law, his boss and eventually two of his daughters. The third daughter is alive even though she was slashed across her throat.

The same week in northern California, 13-year-old Jennifer Moore headed to the corner ice cream store for a treat. She never came back. Police found her nude body four days later in a garbage bag along the road. Scott Williams, a deacon and Sunday School teacher at her church, confessed to raping Jennifer in the church library, then choking her before he killed her with a baseball bat. Williams had a history of running up hundreds of dollars of phone bills in 976 "dial-a-porn" numbers (it costs when someone calls a 976 telephone number).

Pornography can kill: it really can! Police officer Darrell Pope of the Michigan State Police told how a 17 year-old boy was found hanging in his closet by his father. He was wearing his mom's girdle, underpants, bra and nylon stockings. Around his neck was her slip tied into a knot and attached to a beam. "It was not a suicide," said officer Pope. "It was an accidental death. At the boy's feet was a magazine telling exactly what he had done. What the material forgot to tell him was that if you press down on the artery in your neck with over four pounds of pressure, you will go unconscious. Once he was unconscious he couldn't stand up and he just hung himself."

Sometimes, it just takes one man's story—told in his own words—to explain the harm that pornography does. Here is part of a letter that was received shortly after Dr. James Dobson talked with Ted Bundy:

> I, too, started out looking at girlie magazines, as Ted Bundy did, and finding magazines and pictures of nude women. Then I ran into paperback books about sex, and what started out as interest and excitement turned into a hunger and an addiction. I had to have it and it made me depressed.
>
> I am almost 40 now, and most of my life has been spent thinking about or dreaming about sex. It has touched every important relationship in my life, my mental health, as well as my mind, my work, and worst of all, my spiritual life. My addiction spread from looking at pictures to going to bookstores to seeing videos and movies.
>
> Then I went from a "peeping tom," looking through windows, to showing my private parts to

others. I've spent hours in the night looking for naked people to watch. I've left work for hours to go to bookstores. In crowded shopping malls, I've done or said things to women just to get a thrill. I've spent hundreds of dollars making telephone calls on porn-line calls and probably thousands on films, videos and books.

I had to take time off from work to enter a treatment program for those who can't stop thinking about and having sex. It cost me a marriage and the loss of loved ones and friends. My mind is not my own. I am constantly bothered by the thousands of pornographic images I have fed into my mind over the years.

…Up until a few years ago, there was nowhere I could go for help. I tried. I have spent thousands of dollars on treatment from ungodly mental doctors and counselors who tried to help me become comfortable watching pornography in safe and protected places. That's like trying to teach an alcoholic to drink one or two drinks.

Since receiving treatment for my addiction and turning over all of my life and will to God through Christ, things have improved in a big way. However, I am a walking wounded and scarred person. Even though there is healing going on, I still must face the temptation and desires I have invited into my life. I never knew then what I was asking for.

...You must tell the nation what they are asking for by letting pornography fill their minds. The country is becoming filled with sexual addicts who cannot help but act out the part. Bundy's crimes—as terrible as they were—are only the tip of the iceberg. Consider the thousands of thousands, of people who have had sex with someone in their family, been raped, have sexual diseases like AIDS and who have terrible problems with their feelings.

A Time for Action

All of the above stories—as they are—still won't prove to some "freedom-loving" people that pornography is harmful. They refuse to believe that these things are harmful and have caused many crimes.

The average citizen, however, isn't waiting for more proof. Neither are such leaders as U.S. Senator Mitch McConnell of Kentucky. He presented a bill to the U.S. Congress that would allow victims of sex crimes to sue the makers and sellers of pornography. This would be possible if the person can prove that the bad material affected him or caused him to commit the crime. (That is, if the victim is still alive to sue them.)

According to Senator McConnell, the link between pornography and sex violence is becoming more and more clear. "As young people are being exposed to this vile material at an earlier and earlier age, the number of young people who do sexual crimes is growing—at an alarming rate. We see terrible things like the "wilding" gang rape of a young woman in [New York's] Central Park and the rape of a handicapped girl in New Jersey by five teenagers. We have to ask: How do young people get the idea for such crimes? The answer lies in the pornography that is freely available."

...Somehow, some way, decent-minded people in our society will find a lawful way to stop the poison we see through our eyes that makes men go crazy and commit sexual violence. We do not have to give room for that much "freedom." We do not have to put up with the seeds of ruin being sown at almost every corner store.

The point is not that the human body is evil, or that sex is to be something that's "hush hush." We're not saying that sex in marriage is ugly. God made male and female to be attracted to each other. But that attraction is healthy only when it is limited to respect and commitment and free will in marriage.

When a man has "sex" on his mind and tries to take what no woman will give him freely, then society has a right to check out what started the flame. Arson has never been allowed in our culture. The sexual arson lighted by pornography must be treated like fire.

Do we know for sure that pornography is habit-forming and makes a person want more and more? No, but with the proof that we have, we know enough to stay far away from it. We also know enough to ask our society to dump it...for the safety of us all.

PORN: THE DESTROYER OF LIVES

by Craig Stephen Smith

There is another destroyer of the Indian way of life besides alcohol. It too is habit-forming and self-pleasing and it is spreading across our reservations. Pornography is what it is called. In this article we will call it "porn."

To some, porn makes them think of pictures of women wearing little or nothing. Usually they are standing or lying down in sexual poses. To others, it is the abuse of children who are forced to do sexual things. In some cases films are made of children doing these things and then the pictures are sold. Whatever porn means to you, the result is clear. Porn destroys both those who are abused and those who do the abusing.

Most of the dirty-picture business has grown at a very fast pace. Sales add up to billions of dollars. During 1985 and 1986, the U.S. Attorney General's Commission on Pornography held public hearings across America. They found things like this:

- Children between the ages of 12 and 17 buy most of the dirty pictures.
- These pictures are showing hatred against people of another color. They are violent and make fun of women in particular.
- Many cases of family violence and abuse happen because parents watched and read porn.
- Many young people die each year from doing things they see in these porn movies and magazines.

There is too much to talk about in this article. The report from the Attorney General's Commission took nearly 2000 pages just to tell a little of what it learned.

One thing is very clear about dirty sex pictures and stories. They have a powerful, habit-forming effect on the person who is trapped by them. What begins as a brief look into an interesting magazine usually leads into a craving for more. In the end the pleasure begins to fade. What was once just a glance at a picture, now becomes a terrible habit. What they used to hate becomes hungry monsters inside crying out to be fed.

Porn has many ways to feed that monster. Some of the ways are:

- *Obscene videos.* Citizen magazine called unlawful, dirty videos the fastest growing problem in the 1980s and 90s. Across the United States video stores are big business. Rentals made more than $4 billion in sales last year. This is 60 percent more than movie theatres took in. A survey was taken of junior high students in New York City. It showed that 70 percent of the students had watched dirty-sex videos during one school year.

- *X-rated Stores and Peep Shows.* Many communities still have "sex stores" with "peep show" booths. These are stalls where many times people do dangerous sex acts. They know about AIDS but do not seem to care.

- *X-rated Pornography Through the Mail.* There has been a great increase in X-rated pictures going through the mail. The people who send this material do not try to control who gets it. This is against the law.

- *Dial-a-Porn.* Over the last few years this new problem has attacked our young people and adults. Thousands of people, including children, spend millions of dollars on "phone sex."

- *Child Porn.* Using children to make dirty sex pictures remains a serious nightmare for North America. In one community a postal inspector is trying to bring a stop to it. By himself he is writing to more than 100 people who have broken the law and need help.

   The most unthinkable acts are being forced upon innocent children. Many are being videotaped by these evil men. Then they turn around and sell their tapes to people all across North America and in other countries. Many people get excited and fill their sexual needs by watching children doing sex acts.

- *World-Wide Web/Internet.* With the press of a few keys on a computer, pornography is easily available right at home. Many of these can be saved to the computer's memory and/or printed in full color. There is no charge for accessing the samples presented by the suppliers of these pictures. Opportunity to join a club for a small fee is offered.

Porn is a problem that Native people throughout

North America need to deal with. It is totally destroying our cultural values to see our children being used by adults in such a way. This problem can be as dangerous as alcohol. We don't see it as openly on our reservations as the alcohol problem, but I am convinced it is there.

Porn comes into our Indian villages in all the ways just mentioned as well as by satellite. The filth of dirty-sex pictures is spread through Native homes everywhere by means of their television sets. More and more video stores are springing up on our reservations. Many of these offer porn-type videos. Of course, Native people living in cities have the same sex stores and peep shows available to the general public. Many buy these materials and hide them in their homes to look at later.

The unsatisfied desires of a person caught up in watching and reading porn can be very harmful. Many are not satisfied until they have abused their partner or child. It is a proven fact that many child abusers today are hooked on porn, especially child porn.

What can we do? This huge problem needs to be hit head-on.

We need to see that the laws are kept and that stronger laws are made. Tribal government leaders must face this problem too. One way is to block the flow of pornographic books, videos and magazines into our reservations. Above all else, those who are caught in the grips of porn need to know that there is help available.

As a Native Christian I recognize that this is a spiritual problem. Man's sinful state is clearly shown in the life of a person caught in the grip of porn. For such a person there is forgiveness and a new life through a personal faith in Jesus Christ.

For the child who has been abused there is hope for you. So many of the children who are abused end up with no hope and no future. Often they feel suicide is their only way out but there is an answer! There is only One who can love you in the way true love was supposed to be shown. That one is Jesus Christ. He says, *Come to Me, all of you who work and have heavy loads. I will give you rest* (Matthew 11:23 NLB).

It does not matter if you are the victim or the abuser, there can only be one answer for this problem. If nothing is done, porn will destroy a person in the end and maybe a lot of innocent people as well.

The good news is that there is another road you can take. I invite you to turn from your ways and trust in Christ as your Savior. Ask Him to forgive and cleanse you. Remember, there is hope for you!

PERSONAL STORIES OF THOSE
WHO HAVE STRUGGLED
WITH PORN AND WON

Confessions of a Video Addict

If I could get rid of things I have looked at and undo some of things I have done, I think I'd be a lot happier. I'm thirty-six years old. For over sixteen years I was an addict.

No, I wasn't a drunk. I wasn't addicted to drugs. Glue sniffing wasn't my thing either. But I am an ex-addict.

It began when I was ten. What happened wasn't something I had planned. It just happened.

Leaving the reservation was always exciting. My family and I would make two trips each year to the city of Winnipeg, Manitoba, 600 miles from our northern community. I always looked forward to those trips on the train.

"Come on, James!" my father would say, as he tugged at my sleeve. "It's time to go." I didn't need any reminders or encouragement. I was out of bed in a flash!

The trip used to take us two days on the old rail line that ran from Churchill to Thompson and then down to Winnipeg, the capital of Manitoba.

Mom always packed a lunch. There were no dining cars on those old trains. You either brought what you ate or you didn't eat.

One summer day we set off for Winnipeg. Little did I know that it would be my last train ride for a long, long time.

My parents didn't tell us kids that we were being sent to live with our uncle in Winnipeg. Times were bad in those days and my folks couldn't afford to raise all five kids. So my uncle offered to take us. It was five long years before I saw my house and my dog again.

Things that happened at my uncle's place weren't the best. Some of them I can't repeat. It was during those days of living with Uncle Frank and going to public school in Winnipeg that I became an addict.

I was addicted to something just as strong as alcohol or sniffing glue. My uncle helped me to become an addict.

You see, Uncle Frank was a wild fellow. He was married but the wife he was living with was his third. Uncle Frank didn't have a clean mind. He was addicted to dirty magazines and sex programs on television.

It didn't take long before my brothers and I found some of those dirty pictures. Uncle Frank used to stuff them in the bottom drawer of his desk or under the couch in the sitting room. We didn't have any trouble finding them and he didn't seem to mind when we looked at them. Uncle Frank and his wife used to laugh and think it was funny. When I'd look at pictures of naked women they seemed to think it was OK. I guess they enjoyed watching me stare wide-eyed at the photos.

It was fun for a while but after I had looked at everything I could find, I wanted more. My uncle would bring home a new magazine about once a week. It didn't take me long to finish looking.

This continued for two or three years. Then things seemed to change.

When I turned twelve I discovered I could do some of the things I saw people doing in the pictures. It seems that that was thought of as something natural, to go from dirty pictures to playing around with myself.

It was like I was addicted to alcohol or heroin. In my "sex dreams" I picked the kind of girls I wanted to be with.

During the middle of my teen years I didn't just look at the pictures. I read the articles too. I guess this helped me to think and do sexual things.

My brothers looked at the magazines but they didn't seem to be affected by them the same way: I really couldn't tell. You see, the youngest of my brothers was three years older than I was. They always were going out with the girls. I didn't know what they did but I'm sure those dirty pictures had a lot to do with the way they acted.

During the last year that I lived with Uncle Frank I met a girl who later became my wife. She was the most beautiful girl I had ever known. She had the kind of body I had come to love through the pages of those magazines. Even though I was just sixteen, we were already sleeping together: we were not married. We didn't get married until I was nineteen; she was seventeen.

After a couple of years our marriage didn't seem to be fun any more. It didn't satisfy my desires. I wanted more of what I saw.

Then something happened that almost tore our marriage apart.

On a trip to Vancouver my friend introduced me to a video store. I hadn't been to one before. I wish I never saw this one. This trip started me down a path that brought happiness for a while, but it was tearing my wife and me apart.

Shortly after my Vancouver trip I started ordering videos from British Columbia. They'd come about once a week. I soon found myself watching these pictures almost every day. A year or so later, a video store opened in Winnipeg. I would go and use the private booths. While looking at the movies I would act out what I saw.

It didn't take long before I was no longer satisfied at home. I wanted my wife to be like those models in the movies. With two children and another one on the way she just didn't quite fit the part.

I threatened to walk out on her if she didn't satisfy my needs the way I wanted. Thank God, her beauty was not only her body, but also her spirit. Even though she refused to do what I wanted she stuck with me.

She could tell that I was sick and she wanted to help me.

My wife put up with my dirty sex magazines in the house. She also stood by me when I would stay out until one and two o'clock in the morning acting out my desires in the video booth. I also had another girl or two but my wife didn't give up.

About a year after I got married my wife started going to church. Her mother took her to one down the street from where she lived. My wife didn't have to hear very many Bible stories before she asked the teacher how she could become a child of God. Now that she was a Christian my wife was just what I needed to keep our lives together and to put my feet on the right path.

My addiction continued until my oldest child began school. During her first school year I came to know the Living God through a gospel crusade in Winnipeg. After the message the preacher gave an invitation to accept Jesus Christ and find freedom from the chains that bound me.

I went forward. The counselor was so helpful. He showed me that when Christ comes into our lives, He washes all our sins away. That means all the things we have done even when we were children. When I left the meeting that night I felt such joy. I knew I had found the way to solve my problem.

After I came to know the Lord I really wanted to get rid of all those magazines. Most of all I wanted to get rid of "dirty thoughts" that ran through my mind every day. I wanted to get rid of the chains that had bound me for almost sixteen years.

I knew I was not strong enough to do it myself. I needed God's help. I can't begin to thank Him for my wife and my children. They stood by me during all these terrible times.

It took almost three years to be completely free. I saw God do a lot of wonderful things for me during this time but it was very hard.

My first victory was getting rid of my magazines. It took me almost two years to stop going to "sex bookstores" and video stores. With God's help I was also able to stop seeing my "lady friends" and having sex with myself.

The book of Proverbs in the Bible has some strong, helpful words for young men. It says,

> *Now then, my sons, listen to me. Do not turn away from the words of my mouth. Keep far away from her* [a street woman and pornography]. *Do not go near the door of her house. If you do, you would give your strength to others, and your years to those without lovingkindness...You would cry inside yourself when your end comes, when your flesh and body are wasted away* [from STDs or AIDS].

This book also gives advice for husbands. It tells us to

> *Drink water from your own pool, flowing water from your own well...Let them be yours alone and not for strangers with you...be happy with the wife you married when you were young...Be filled with great joy always because of her love. My son, why should you be carried away with a sinful woman* [or sex magazines] *and fall into the arms of a strange woman* [or a sex video store]?

> *For the ways of a man are seen by the eyes of the Lord, and He watches all his paths. His own sins will trap the sinful. He will be held with the ropes of his sin. He will die for want of teaching, and will go the wrong way because of the greatness of his foolish ways* (Proverbs 5:15-23 NLB).

What's Happened to Me?
by Kari Hill

Mike left the video party in disgust. The other guys were too caught up in the movie to notice him go.

"How can they enjoy something like that?" Mike thought. "An X-rated movie—it's garbage!"

Mike rubbed his eyes as if to wipe the terrible scenes from his mind. It didn't help. He decided to walk the long way home hoping it would clear his head.

As he walked the young man observed that lights were still on in most of the houses he passed. "Not uncommon for midnight," he thought, "especially on the weekend." Parties would go until the early morning hours around here. Mike also noticed the TVs glowing in some of the living rooms. This reminded him of the situation he had just come from.

"What's happened to me?" he wondered to himself. "I used to be like all the other guys. I knew watching those kinds of programs was wrong but I watched them anyway. There was a kind of excitement in doing something that wasn't right. But that was before I decided to follow Jesus. Now I don't feel right watching those videos. To tell the truth, they seem dirtier than ever. It's like I know Jesus is watching too, and He isn't pleased with that type of thing."

The troubled teen paused in his thoughts as a nearby pack of coyotes began their evening howling ritual. Almost immediately the dogs on the reserve joined in with their yipping.

"Crazy mutts," Mike muttered to himself.

"What am I gonna do?" Mike's thoughts had returned to his problem. "I know I can't watch those movies anymore but what will I say to the guys? What will they say to me? They'll laugh me right out of school. How can I say 'no' when they're all forcing me to watch those dirty videos? I don't want to lose my friends!"

Mike worried the whole way home. When he reached the front of his house he got an answer to his questions.

"Pray. That's it!" Mike thought. "Joe, the Bible man, said that's the first thing I should do when I have a problem: pray."

Mike looked up into the sky. He could always picture God better that way. He quietly spoke, "Lord, I-uh-still don't know how to talk to You very good. I've only been living for You about a month. But-uh-I need your help. I'm scared to say 'no' to my friends. I know I have to. Please make me bold. Let the gang some day understand why I can't and won't watch those videos. Forgive me for watching that stuff in the first place. Thank you. Amen."

Mike looked around him. No one was around and it was quiet outside. But he knew God had heard his prayer. He felt better.

All the next week the determined teen managed to turn down his friends' invitation to their video parties. He even handled their teasing and words like "Mike's gone religious" as best he could.

He had another problem bothering him now. It was the bad movies he had already seen. He couldn't get them out of his mind. He didn't want to remember them but they wouldn't leave his thoughts. During the night and all through the day they were like filthy monsters attacking his mind.

Mike was getting very frustrated. He didn't know how to get rid of those thoughts. He thought of going to see his friend, Bible Joe. Joe had told him to come to him if ever he needed to talk about anything. Mike trusted Joe. He was a kind man in his twenties. Joe always seemed to have an answer for Mike's difficult questions. But Mike felt too embarrassed to tell Joe about this.

When these horrible thoughts kept running through his mind Mike decided to see Joe. It took a lot of stammering. He beat around the bush but Mike, with his red face, finally got it out.

"Joe, I've seen lots of dirty videos in the last few months. I can't seem to get them out of my mind. What can I do?"

Bible Joe was an understanding fellow. He didn't frown at what Mike told him. He had heard that story before.

After thinking quietly for a moment, Joe replied, "You are wise to say 'no' to those videos, Mike. It won't do you any good to keep on cluttering your mind with garbage. You know, once something gets into your memory it never leaves."

"Does this mean I'm always gonna have these thoughts?" Mike asked. He was really worried.

"It's always going to be there but it doesn't have to be in your everyday thoughts," Joe replied. "You see, some of these things slip into the back of your brain. They are put into something like a storage place. These are things you don't think about every day."

"How can I make this happen, Joe?"

"Well, you don't want to think bad thoughts anymore, right?"

"You bet."

"Then start thinking of good things, of anything that is pure and right and you know who the best One to think about is don't you?"

"Yes, Jesus."

"Listen to this," Joe said as he reached for his Bible,

Keep your minds thinking about whatever is true, whatever is respected, whatever is right, whatever is pure, whatever can be loved, and whatever is well thought of. If there is anything good and worth giving thanks for, think about these things" (Philippians 4:8).

"So you need to fill your mind with His Word," continued Joe. "Memorize verses. And more importantly..."

"Pray," Mike said, taking the word out of his mouth. "You know, Joe, I have been so concerned about this that I haven't prayed like I should have. I'm gonna start. Thanks, Joe! Appreciate it!"

Friend, you have seen the battle Mike had, and will keep on having. All because he watched something he shouldn't have. Our video and TV watching is no joke! Please think twice before you watch. Your brain is not like a chalkboard. You can't just erase something you don't like. The mind holds all information, good and bad. The way each of us acts depends on what we have on our minds.

Be careful! Learn to say "no" to wrong things. Let Jesus help you to get rid of bad thoughts. He is the only One who can!

List of writers and contributors to PORNOGRAPHY topic:

Mike Yorkey and Dean Merrill - This article is adapted from an article printed in *Focus on the Family Magazine,* October 1989. Copyright 1989, Focus on the Family, Pomona, CA 91799. All Rights Reserved. Used by permission.

Dr. Jerry R. Kirk – adapted from *The Power of the Picture.* ©1989. National Coalition for the Protection of Children and Families. Used by Permission.

CHAPTER SEVEN

Does the Power of Solvent Addiction Still Hold You in Its Grip?

ADDICTION RIGHT UNDER OUR NOSES

by Jim Uttley

North America is faced with a serious crisis. It's not El Niño, La Niña or global warming. This crisis surrounds us, yet very few of us are aware of how lethal it is. The crisis is solvent abuse, also known as "inhalant abuse." You will be amazed and horrified when you learn about this serious threat to our children, teens and young adults.

"More than one million youth tried inhalants in a recent one-year period. An estimated 660,000 users tried inhalants for the first time in 1994, up from 428,000 in 1991" (U.S. Substance Abuse and Mental Health Services Administration's [SAMSHA] *Household Survey*).

In their lifetime, more than 12 million people ages 12 and older have tried "huffing" (breathing through the mouth) correction fluid, glue, gasoline, spray paint and many other dangerous products that potentially cause brain damage or even death.

There is another dangerous trend. Since 1991, lifetime inhalant usage has shot up from 17.6% of 8th graders using inhalants to 21.6%; 15.7% of 10th graders to 19%; and, 17.6% of 12th graders to 19.4%.

The reason that inhalants are popular is simple: they are inexpensive, available and legal to buy. Young people have been warned to look out for alcohol, tobacco and other drugs but not many know that sniffing correction fluid, gasoline, felt-tip markers, spray paint, typewriter correction fluid, air-conditioning refrigerant, air freshener, butane, cooking spray or glue can kill them or damage them physically and mentally.

When it comes to solvent abuse, Aboriginals in particular, are once again being oppressed and exploited by those in the dominant society. For example, in Winnipeg, with its large Aboriginal population, it is extremely difficult if not impossible for Natives to walk into a hardware store and buy a jar of rubber cement or a can of lacquer. But these items are extremely easy to get on the streets from non-Aboriginal "pushers." In spite of severe fines and penalties, trafficking in solvent abuse is high. On remote reservations in the U.S. and Canada, people are taking advantage of others' addictions and through their greed are becoming rich while keeping their "customers" in poverty and despair.

Surveys are not very accurate when it comes to Native American rates of solvent abuse. Nor are they accurate in determining causes of death. Deaths of inhalant abusers may be listed as "undetermined" on a death certificate because a specific screening test for inhalants was not part of an autopsy. For this reason, inhalants as either the main cause or a contributing factor in a death are not always reported, especially at the national level.

"Deaths are sometimes listed as undetermined if good toxicology has not been done," said Suzanne Dana, Deputy Medical Examiner for Travis County in Texas.

Most rural areas and smaller cities do not have labs that are able to determine if inhalants were a cause of death, according to James C. Garriot, chief toxicologist with the Bexar County Forensic Science Center. Tragically, treatment facilities for inhalant users are rare and difficult to find. Users suffer a high rate of relapse and require thirty to forty days or more of treatment which is expensive.

What can we do to stop the assault on our people?

- Become informed. Education is the key to preventing a child's deadly mistake.

- Educate yourself.

- Educate your family. Talk to your children about the dangers of Inhalant Abuse. If you contact the National Inhalant Prevention Coalition (In the U.S.: 800-269-4237; In Canada: 512-480-8953).

- Contact your local officials to learn what programs they have in place to educate and prevent solvent abuse. Support your local law enforcement officers in helping them stem the abuse and killing.

- If you are a retailer, get a list of the solvents and refuse to sell them to anyone under 18. If necessary, ask for identification.

- If you live in an area where there are a lot of solvent abusers, get involved in the local outreach programs for these broken people. A few churches reach out to solvent abusers and alcoholics. If there is no outreach in your area, consider starting one.

Sniffers are considered the lowest of the poor and outcasts, especially among our First Nations. Listen to them. Befriend them. Show them love and care. Show them that we are people who want them to find healing and wholeness.

COMMUNITIES DISTURBED BY
SOLVENT ADDICTION

Solvent abuse is fast becoming as poignant a symbol of the turmoil in Canada's Aboriginal communities as dilapidated houses and rampant unemployment. But there remains a determined optimism among some that communities of First Nations people can learn to help themselves.

On November 24, 1997, the CHAMP House, a shelter for homeless youth in Hyannis, Massachusetts, was destroyed by a massive blaze that started when two residents inhaled propane and lit a cigarette. Both boys suffered injuries. While the seventeen-year-old recovered shortly after the fire, the nineteen-year-old suffered burns over 45 percent of his body.

When flames tore through the East Dayton, Ohio home of three huffers, toluene and other paints in the apartment helped ignite a blaze that could not be controlled. Perhaps the outcome of the fire would not have been lethal if the three victims, all in their mid-30s, had not been under the influence of toluene, a powerful industrial solvent used in paints and adhesives and often misused to get high.

In Davis Inlet, a remote Labrador Innu community that has attracted international attention because of rampant gas-sniffing, a large number of youths, some as young as seven, went on a gasoline-induced rampage through the community, broke windows, trashed a school classroom, threw paint at several buildings and damaged a police vehicle. There has been an alarming increase in solvent abuse in most of Canada's 55 Inuit communities in the last five years.

"It's all very upsetting," said Okalik Eegeesiak, president of the Inuit Tapirisat, which represents 45,000 Inuit in Quebec, Newfoundland and the Arctic. "It's sad when people think they have no opportunities in their communities." Solvent abuse has led to more suicides, domestic abuse and other violent crime. She blames overcrowded, poorly built homes, a lack of economic development, and an inability to wrestle control of health and social programs away from the federal government.

Expectations are high that Ottawa's response to the 1996 Royal Commission on Aboriginal Peoples will lead to tangible change. But Eegeesiak said it's difficult to stay patient and wait for the much-needed money to make those changes possible. "It's bad when people have local solutions that require national decisions and the resources aren't there for them to control it themselves." For the 500 residents of Davis Inlet, the federal government has taken the drastic measure of funding an $85-million relocation to nearby Little Sango Pond.

Jane Stewart, former Indian Affairs Minister of Canada, said the government has tried to work more closely with the community's leaders and other federal departments to develop a common strategy and be more effective in the fight to reduce solvent abuse. "It's a complex issue obviously, and it's going to take all our best efforts," Stewart said from Ottawa.

Rahael Jahan, a professor at the Saskatchewan Indian Federated College at the University of Regina, said, "There's no question that there's a difficulty here with deep roots. We are all challenged to understand the complexities [of] the legacy of the past and the impacts on the present. Years of inaction by previous governments have only added to those complexities, which for many include generations of physical and sexual abuse. The problem was created, and needs to be addressed, at the government level." Jahan heads a study into the low ratio of Aboriginal students in areas such as medicine. "But," she stressed, "money alone isn't the answer. The right programs must be chosen to give Aboriginal communities better access to education and treatment for substance abuse and sniffing. The problems First Nations communities face are so overwhelming. The sense of frustration that results is because people don't know where to start."

INHALANT ABUSE IS DEADLY

There is no typical profile for an inhalant abuser. Victims are represented by both sexes and all socioeconomic groups throughout the U.S. It's not unusual to see elementary and middle school age youths involved with inhalant abuse.

There are many scenarios of how young people die of inhalant abuse. Here are three of them:

A 13 year-old boy was inhaling fumes from cleaning fluids and became ill a few minutes afterwards. Witnesses alerted the parents and the victim was hospitalized and placed on life support systems. He died 24 hours after the incident.

An 11 year-old boy collapsed in a public bathroom. A butane cigarette lighter fuel container and a plastic bag were found next to him. He also had bottles of typewriter correction fluid in his pocket. CPR was applied but he did not revive and was pronounced dead.

A 15 year-old boy was found unconscious in a backyard. According to three companions, the four teenagers had taken gas from a family's grill propane tank. They put the gas in a plastic bag and inhaled the gas to get high. The victim collapsed shortly after inhaling the gas. He died on the way to the hospital.

Inhaling fumes from products like hairspray, nail polish, model glue, and spray paint is so popular, nearly one in five kids has done it by eighth grade. It's even as popular as marijuana. And anytime these products are huffed they can kill.

- Products that are abused, when used as designed are legal, useful and serve many needs in our community.
- There is an almost endless supply of products that can be used as inhalants—over 1,000.
- Products are available at home, school, grocery and auto supply stores.
- Some products are free or inexpensive in comparison to illegal drugs.
- Laws against selling inhalants to minors are difficult to enforce, as these products are not illegal. The punishment is minimal.
- No complex equipment is needed to abuse these inhalants.
- Young people do not have to go to a dealer to purchase their products. They can find the stuff almost anywhere.
- People can abuse the products practically anywhere, as they are easy to hide.
- It is difficult to detect if someone is using inhalants. One exception would be the use of glue. Its smell tends to "stick" with the person.
- Educational and awareness programs are not available in many schools and communities.
- Adults are generally unaware of the symptoms and have no idea that their children may be sniffing or huffing inhalants.
- Sniffers and huffers are generally unaware of the consequences of their actions and many just don't care.

Inhalant use refers to the intentional breathing of gas or vapors with the purpose of reaching a high. Inhalants are legal, everyday products which have a useful purpose, but can be misused.

Experimenting with inhalants is widespread among teenagers. In studies done among eighth, tenth, and twelfth grades, the use of inhalants was only surpassed by the use of marijuana, cigarette and alcohol.

There is a public belief that inhalant abuse is more common among Aboriginal youth than among other ethnic groups. The rates among Aboriginal youth are very high, second only to that of Caucasian youth.

Abusing the products brings effects which slow down the body's function. Depending on how much the abuser inhales, he or she can experience slight stimulation, feeling of less inhibition or loss of consciousness. The user can also suffer from Sudden Sniffing Death Syndrome. This means the user can die the first, tenth, or one-hundredth time he or she uses an inhalant. Other effects include damage to the heart, kidney, brain, liver, bone marrow and other organs. The effects of inhalant abuse during pregnancy are very similar to Fetal Alcohol Syndrome. Inhalants are physically and psychologically addictive and users suffer withdrawal symptoms, sometimes much greater and more difficult to overcome than recovering from heroin or cocaine addiction.

How do Inhalants work in the body?

The prolonged use of solvents entails significant risk of brain damage to the user. Other serious health problems observed in chronic sniffers include breathing difficulties, liver malfunction, kidney and blood abnormalities. Abnormalities appear to be reversible when the individual stops using the inhalants. However, brain and nervous system damage can be permanent. Other dangers include Sudden Sniffing Death, violent or aggressive behavior, suffocation, burns and freezing to death. Some studies have also identified fetal solvent syndrome in children born to women who use solvents during pregnancy.

The strength of these effects depends on the experience and personality of the user, how much is taken, the specific substance inhaled, and the user's surroundings. The high from inhalants tends to be short or can last several hours if used repeatedly.

- Although different in makeup, nearly all of the abused inhalants produce effects similar to anesthetics, which act to slow down the body's functions.

- At low doses, users may feel slightly stimulated; at higher amounts they may feel less inhibited, less in control; at high doses, a user can lose consciousness.

- Initial effects include: nausea, sneezing, coughing, nosebleeds, feeling and looking tired, bad breath, lack of coordination, loss of appetite.

Why is abuse of this drug a problem?
- Deep breathing of the vapors or using much over a short period of time, may result in losing touch with

one's surroundings, a loss of self-control, violent behavior, unconsciousness, or death. Using inhalants can cause nausea and vomiting. If a person is unconscious when vomiting occurs, death can result from aspiration.

- Sniffing highly concentrated amounts of solvents or aerosol sprays can produce heart failure and instant death. Sniffing can cause death the first time or any time. High concentrations of inhalants cause death from suffocation by replacing the oxygen in the lungs. Inhalants also can cause death by depressing the central nervous system so much that breathing slows down until it stops.

- Death from inhalants is usually caused by a very high concentration of inhalant fumes. Deliberately inhaling from a paper bag greatly increases the chances of suffocation. Even when using aerosol or volatile (vaporous) products for their legitimate purposes, such as, painting, cleaning, etc., it is wise to do so in a well-ventilated room or outdoors.

- Long-term use can cause weight loss, fatigue, electrolyte (salt) imbalance, and muscle fatigue. Repeated sniffing of concentrated vapors over a number of years can cause permanent damage to the nervous system, which means greatly reduced physical and mental capabilities. In addition, long-term sniffing of certain inhalants can damage the liver, kidneys, blood, and bone marrow.

- Tolerance, which means the sniffer needs more and more each time to get the same effect, is likely to develop from most inhalants when they are used regularly.

- As in all drug use, taking more than one drug at a time multiplies the risks. Using inhalants while taking other drugs that slow down the body's functions, such as tranquilizers, sleeping pills, or alcohol, increases the risk of death from overdose. Loss of consciousness, coma, or death can result.

Following a peak in inhalant use two years ago, government surveys now show that the number of young people using solvents has taken a slight dip. However, overall inhalant usage statistics remain largely unchanged.

The 1997 National Institute on Drug Abuse (NIDA) Monitoring the Future Survey reports that, by the eighth grade, one in five kids—21.0%, down from 21.2% in 1996, will have used inhalants to get high at the risk of brain damage and even death.

Results of the NIDA study come as the Office of National Drug Control Policy (ONDCP) has announced a $195 million dollar advertising campaign to persuade kids to stay away from drugs, particularly gate-way drugs such as marijuana and inhalants.

Other government studies show similar trends in inhalant use. The National Household Survey on Drug Abuse, published by the Substance Abuse and Mental Health Services Administration (SAMHSA), indicates that the number of individuals who reported using inhalants in their lifetime dropped from an estimated 12,016,000 individuals in 1995 to 11,909,000 in 1996. SAMHSA reports that in the United States during 1995 there were approximately 676,000 new inhalant users, up from 401,000 in 1991. Findings also show that increases have occurred in the number of persons reporting use during the past month and past year. Past year use increased in the age 12 and older bracket and in the 17 and older bracket.

The most common products used include:

- Age 12 to 17—(1) glue, shoe polish and toluene; (2) gasoline or lighter fluid; and (3) nitrous oxide ("whippets")

- Age 18 to 25—(1) nitrous oxide; (2) gasoline or lighter fluid; and (3) amyl nitrite ("poppers"), Locker Room odorizers, or Rush

- Age 26 to 34—(1) amyl nitrite ("poppers"), Locker Room odorizers, or Rush; (2) nitrous oxide ("whippets"), and (3) glue, shoe polish and toluene

- Age 35 and older—(1) amyl nitrite ("poppers"), Locker Room odorizers, or Rush; (2) nitrous oxide ("whippets"), and (3) glue, shoe polish and toluene.

FIRST NATIONS AND INUIT
SOLVENT ABUSE

The coincidence could not have been more horrible.

On November 20, 1998, in Shamattawa, an isolated Cree reserve 650 kilometers north of Winnipeg, RCMP (Royal Canadian Mounted Police) Sergeant Len Hordijk sat at a meeting in the Native band's office describing the epidemic of solvent abuse among the community's youth. Sgt. Hordijk was recounting how children on the reserve, some as young as eight years old, are addicted to sniffing gasoline when a band member burst into the room, said something in Cree, and bolted out. Two councilors followed him.

The officer appeared to be puzzled for a moment, then continued speaking. Eric Robinson suddenly interrupted him. (Eric is the reserve's NDP MLA — New Democratic Party Member of the Legislative Assembly — and a Cree from Cross Lake, Manitoba.)

"Sir, it appears that we have just had a homicide," Mr. Robinson said, his voice and hands starting to shake. "A young boy has been shot by another youth and sniffing was involved."

Sgt. Hordijk stood from his chair and rushed to the scene, a house with a boarded up front door in the middle of the town of 850. A 14 year-old boy lay dead in the yard behind two trucks, only his feet showing from under a blanket.

RCMP said the victim was Charles Redhead and that an 18 year-old was charged with second-degree murder. Sgt. Hordijk said both youths were high on solvents but wouldn't comment further. Community leaders said the two are brothers.

"Both of them are sniffing and one of them went crazy," said former reserve chief, Sam Miles, as he watched police cordon off the family's home.

On the front steps of a neighboring house, a woman, huddled in blankets, sat and sobbed quietly. A man on a four-wheel ATV tore away from the home, obviously distraught, pounding the handlebars with his fists.

"I hate to say it, but you almost expect things like this to happen in Shamattawa," Mr. Miles said.

It was a chilling end to a day that band officials had spent explaining the reserve's plight, talking about the astronomical rates of solvent abuse and suicide. Mr. Miles and other officials had invited a group of reporters to the reserve to see the devastation first-hand, hoping to add fuel to their cries for a local solvent abuse treatment center.

Statistics show that at least 120 people on the reserve have either killed themselves or attempted suicide since 1992. An estimated four out of five Shamattawa youths sniff solvents. Housing is desperately short, unemployment is at 85% and food costs are the highest in Manitoba. Eric Robinson compares Shamattawa's problems to Davis Inlet, the Newfoundland reserve that once supplied newscasts with shocking footage of local teens high on gasoline and talking suicide. "I would say that the situation here is as desperate as it was there. It's a community in perpetual crisis," he said.

Earlier in the day, Mr. Robinson, Mr. Miles, a cadre of band councillors and reporters had hopped into pick-ups for a tour. The reserve, at the confluence of the Gods and Echoing Rivers about 100 kilometers south of Hudson bay, is an isolated northern town, accessible only by air in the summer and by roads built across the frozen landscape in winter. Hoarfrost spikes the trees and the dreariness is punctured only by the town's first fire truck, a lime-green relic with no wheels, gently rusting in the ditch. "They sent us that a while ago but it doesn't work any more," Mr. Miles said. The tour starts at the cemetery.

It sits about three kilometers from Shamattawa's gravel-strip airport and is divided into two sections. In the newer half, tiny plaques on the crosses tell the story. The dozens buried here all died since 1996. Most were in their mid-teens and early 20s. It's something like a military graveyard, except nearly everyone here died from their own hand.

"We have the natural deaths on one side and the suicides on the other. We don't want them clashing," said Mr. Miles, an articulate 47-year-old who often acts as the band's spokesman. "When someone commits suicide, it's murder."

The next grim stop on the tour is at a grave which belongs to a 27 year-old woman who walked five kilometers from town into the bush and hung herself from a tree. The tree, according to custom, was burned after the woman's body was cut down. Ashes still surround the fist-sized stump. The small clearing which surrounds it is utterly still and quiet. "You can imagine what went through her mind when she walked out here," Mr. Miles said. "She had a long time to think. It's a long walk."

The morning after the woman's funeral, another woman hung herself, he says. Tragedies in Shamattawa come in terrible bunches.

The next stop is the nursing station, where heart-breaking drawings by children are posted on the wall. One, drawn by an eight year-old girl named Samantha Watt, shows little stick figures splashing in the water. The caption reads: "Swimming is better than sniffing."

On the way back to the band office, Mr. Miles stops at the town's other, older cemetery to visit the grave of his brother Leonard, who died in the early 70s as a 16 year-old boy, Shamattawa's first death from sniffing gasoline. The town's youth recreation center—a graffiti-scarred hut with a lone pool table and a color TV—is named after him.

"There was a lot of lead in the gas back then," Mr. Miles recalled, as he fished through the snow to find Leonard's cross, which has fallen. "People didn't really understand what happened when you sniffed gas. Leonard didn't know until it was too late." He abruptly drops the cross and starts trudging through the snow back to the truck. In a day spent chronicling the misery of his home, it is the closest he comes to breaking down. "It's a sad thing," he says, looking down and brushing the snow from his hands. "It's a constant reminder."

Everybody in Shamattawa knows someone who sniffs. Gasoline is by far the most common solvent abused.

People smuggle cans of hair spray past security checks at the airport and sell them for $80, and bottles of nail polish also fetch big prices. But gas is cheaper and easier to get.

Verna Redhead, who lives a short walk from the band office, knows very well three who sniff. They're her daughters. "I try my best to look after my kids, but I can't get them to stop," she says. "I tell them to sleep and they're up all night with it."

Verna has five girls, each from a different father. One daughter, 18-year-old Laurie, is pretty, with long black hair, tiny glasses and a quick smile. She sniffs gasoline nearly every night. She once went to a solvent abuse treatment center in Thompson, 300 kilometers away, and got clean. But when she came back to Shamattawa, she started abusing again.

"I want to stop, but it's hard," Laurie said. "You see your friends and they go, 'Wanna sniff tonight?' You say no and then they ignore you. There's nothing else happening so you end up sniffing."

Shamattawa's leaders say residents like Laurie Redhead are the reason they're fighting for their own 10-bed treatment center. Without one, they say, abusers will keep coming back to Shamattawa after they're clean and simply fall back into their destructive ways.

Current chief Paddy Massan sent a proposal for the center to the Minister of Indian Affairs and Northern Development. He hasn't had a response.

As Verna starts to talk about how she supports Massan's idea, the bedroom door opens and a young man staggers out. He looks about 20 years old. He reeks of gasoline. Verna waves her hand in front of her face to lessen the stench. She asks who he is but he doesn't answer, only muttering something about gasoline under his breath.

Sam Miles said people seek the brief, euphoric high that sniffing provides in order to escape from Shamattawa's living conditions.

"There are 150 people here who don't have their own houses. Some houses have five or six families in them—three bedroom houses," he said, before listing a further litany of problems.

Power on the reserve is erratic because it comes from a 15-amp diesel generator, a relic of the 1950s. Drinking water has to be hauled from the Gods River because the tap water from wells contains so much methane that it can be ignited if enough pressure builds up in the pipes. And, of course, Shamattawa is isolated, and it's cold. Kids have nothing to do.

All are common laments from isolated Native communities, which makes Mr. Miles wonder if southern Canada is becoming desensitized to them. "I don't know what more we have to do to show people that we need help here," he said. "Not just with the solvent abuse, but with all the things that lead to it." Perhaps the murder of Charles Redhead will prompt some action, he mused.

It quickly became clear Friday afternoon that band leaders and Mr. Robinson will use the homicide to try to compel the government to act. Barely two hours after the slaying, Mr. Robinson's assistant faxed a strongly worded letter mentioning the murder. Band councillors huddle and plot strategy in the office of Chief Massan, who is away in Winnipeg on business.

At day's end, in the office's battered, spartan foyer, a receptionist puts away the moccasins and beads she tried to sell earlier in the day to Shamattawa's visitors from the South. All smiles in the morning, she is now forlorn and near tears, the very picture of numb grief.

One wonders: is she thinking about the tragedy which just occurred or the ones to come?

◆

Meanwhile, in Winnipeg, the body of Marcus Mason, 22, was discovered in a crawl space under an exit ramp in a shopping center garage. Police say Mason was a solvent abuser and may have been dead for three months.

There may be as many as 400 solvent addicts on Winnipeg streets, says a preliminary report by a social service agency. "There isn't an appropriate treatment to respond to the magnitude of the problem we have," says Wayne Helgason, executive director of the Social Planning Council of Winnipeg. "There isn't adequate treatment in either numbers or approach."

The report indicates the majority of solvent abusers are Aboriginal males who have less than a high school diploma, based on 240 addicts in contact with the Addictions Foundation of Winnipeg during 1995-96.

"We need to turn off the tap and [develop] prevention programs on how damaging and dangerous these chemicals are. If we make a difference for one person we're probably saving thousands and thousands of dollars."

The chronic solvent abuser tends to be poor, said Dr. Jay Goldstein, a University of Manitoba sociologist. "Unfortunately, in urban areas in Western Canada, Aboriginals tend to be over-represented in terms of that category," said Goldstein. "It's a way for people to escape from unpleasant circumstances, at least on a temporary basis."

"Young people tend to experiment with solvents but most give it up. Those who do go on to use it on a regular basis run the risk of serious health effects including death. Sniffing solvents causes a temporary feeling of euphoria but side effects include a fast heart rate, excessive anxiety, distortion of reality and violence. Long-term use can lead to brain damage and ultimately death brought on by heart attacks and asphyxiation," said Dr. Arthur Herscovitch, a clinical psychologist with the Addictions Foundation. "But help is available."

The Sagkeeng Solvent Treatment Centre runs a six-month treatment program for Aboriginal youth between ages 13 and 17 from across Canada. The program combines western counselling technique, cultural therapy, and classes. "The idea is to get them back to the mainstream school system once they leave here. We try to teach them some basic skills so that when they leave, they're able to look after themselves much better."

There are currently 36 youth enrolled in the program.

Solvent abuse is an increasing concern in many First Nations and Inuit communities. Studies have shown solvent use is highest where poverty, prejudice and lack of opportunity are common. A number of factors appear to contribute to the use of solvents, including dysfunctional families, alcohol or drug abuse, physical or sexual abuse and poverty.

Most solvent abusers are between the ages of 12 and 19 years old, however there are cases where some have been as young as 8 and as old as their middle 30s. Because of the young age of the abusers and the serious health effects, in Canada, the Minister of Health made prevention and treatment of solvent abuse a health priority in the spring of 1994. At the time, only one permanent First Nation run treatment facility was in operation. Since then, seven new treatment centers have been brought into service at locations across the country as part of a $17.5 million solvent abuse prevention and treatment program. The most recent is in Red Pheasant, Saskatchewan. The programs, which are designed for youths between the ages of 12 and 25 (with most between the ages of 12 and 18), have residencies of six months. They are non-medical and are designed to be culturally relevant.

The First Nations and Inuit Health Program Directorate is currently developing an evaluation framework and accreditation process for the centers. The accreditation process is being pilot-tested and was implemented in April, 1999. A solvent abuse information system was developed in 1997/98 and was completely implemented in 1999.

Retailers Need to Know About Inhalants

Do you consider yourself a drug-pusher? Most likely not. However we would urge you to think again. Inhalants (drugs) are right under our noses. They are legal; they are also lethal. While inhalants have been abused for decades, their popularity as the "drug of choice" is increasing.

Retailers can play a part in stemming the tide of inhalant use by learning about the problem. Educate yourself about your State or Provincial laws and learn how to protect the youth in your community, your store's stock and property.

Tips for Retailers

- Monitor the sale of harmful products to young people and refuse to sell unusual quantities of harmful substances without parental consent. Question young people who buy several containers at a time of glue, rubber cement, spray paint, air freshener, cooking spray, or other inhalable products.

- Watch for minors that regularly buy inhalable products. Note any unusual consumption of certain products, particularly on weekends, and refuse to sell them if you have reason to believe they are being abused.

- Shoplifting inhalable products is a common practice. Keep track of missing products to know if you have sniffers regularly stealing from your store.

- Consider placing abusable products where they can be monitored by store employees.

- Know the laws regarding sale of inhalants to minors.
- Display warning signs and/or prevention posters in a visible area near the cash register.
- Educate your employees, especially at point of sale.
- Talk to the young people in your life about inhalants and let them know the dire consequences of abusing these poisonous chemicals.
- Share this information with other retailers in your area and see what actions can be taken as a group.
- If someone is found huffing on your property, remain calm and do not try to aggravate the user. Inhalant users can experience hallucinations or increased aggression. Also, sudden scares or stress can increase the chance of Sudden Sniffing Death.

Dangerous Solvents

Adhesives: model airplane glue, rubber cement, household glue

Aerosols: spray paint, hairspray, air freshener, deodorant, fabric protector

Solvents & gases: nail polish remover, paint thinner, type correction fluid and thinner, toxic markers, pure toluene, cigar lighter fluid, gasoline, carburetor cleaner, octane booster

Cleaning agents: dry cleaning fluid, spot remover, degreaser

Food products: vegetable cooking spray, dessert topping spray (whipped cream), whippets

Gases: nitrous oxide, butane, propane, helium

Anesthetics

Anesthetic: nitrous oxide, ether, chloroform

Nitrites: Nitrite room odorizers

Amyl: "Poppers," "Snappers"

Butyl: "Rush," "Locker Room," "Bolt," "Climax," also marketed in shops as "video head cleaner"

Two of the most dangerous solvents used are amyl nitrite and butyl nitrite.

- Amyl nitrite is used for heart patients and for diagnostic purposes because it enlarges the blood vessels and makes the heart beat faster.

- Reports of amyl nitrite abuse occurred before 1979 when it was available without a prescription. When it became available by prescription only, many users abused butyl nitrite instead.

- Butyl nitrite is packaged in small bottles and sold under a variety of names, such as "Locker Room" and "Rush." It produces a high that lasts from a few seconds to several minutes. The immediate effects include decreased blood pressure, an increased heart rate, flushed face and neck, dizziness and headache.

The typical user is a teenage male. The National Households Survey on Drug Abuse estimated that 9.1% of 12-17 year-olds and 12.8% of 18-25 year-olds have tried an inhalant at least once.

INHALANT TREATMENT

By the time a student reaches the eighth grade, one in five of his or her peers will have used inhalants to get high. Many young people will become chronic users and require treatment and chemical dependence therapy. Unfortunately, demand for facilities that treat solvent addiction greatly outweighs supply. Chronic inhalant users can and do slip through the cracks.

Can inhalant addiction be treated?

Treatment facilities for sniffing and huffing addicts are rare and difficult to find. Addicts suffer a high rate of relapse and require thirty to forty days or more of withdrawal. Users suffer withdrawal symptoms which can include hallucinations, nausea, excessive sweating, hand tremors, muscle cramps, headaches, chills and delirium tremens. Follow-up treatment is very important.

What To Do When Someone is Huffing

- Remain calm and do not panic.
- Do not excite or argue with the abuser when they are under the influence. They can become aggressive or violent.
- If the person is unconscious or not breathing, call for help. CPR should be administered until help arrives.
- If the person is conscious, keep him or her calm and in a well-ventilated room.
- Excitement or stimulation can cause hallucinations or violence.

- Activity or stress may cause heart problems which may lead to "Sudden Sniffing Death."
- Talk with other persons present or check the area for clues to what was used.
- Once the person is recovered seek professional help for the abuser: school nurse, counselor, physician, other health care worker.
- If use is suspected, adults should be frank but not accusatory in discussions with youth about potential inhalant use.

Inhalant abusers have become a "throw-away" population primarily because few facilities have the necessary experience to treat the compounded medical, neurological and psychological disorders associated with chronic huffers. Furthermore, inhalant abuse is a problem that is largely undertreated by the health care system, understudied by the substance abuse field and overlooked by parents.

"Chronic users do not fit the mold of most drug abuse populations," says Mark Groves (director of the Minneapolis-based Eden Youth Inhalant Abuse & Information Training Project and author of *Preventing Inhalant Abuse: A Training Manual*). "Users are younger, often in trouble with the law, and can suffer medical, psychological and social dysfunction brought on by the chemicals they have sniffed or huffed. Because of the damage neurotoxic chemicals cause to the brain, I think it is wise to consider the regular, chronic inhalant abuser as having a mental health problem rather than a chemical dependency problem. While much of the brain damage from inhalant use is reversible, the process of breaking the chemical dependency and treating the physical and psychological ill-effects of inhalant use takes considerable time. The typical 28-day stay allotted by insurance companies for treatment is inadequate. Experts say it may take at least that amount of time just to get the user ready to engage in therapy. Because neurotoxins are stored in the fatty tissue of the body, the inhalant abuser may experience residual effects for quite some time. This could include altered affect and dullness of intellectual functioning," says Groves.

Detoxification can take 20-30 days and oftentimes much longer. After that, users need either residential treatment or extensive outpatient therapy, often over a year of services and counseling. Insurance companies, however, generally cover just 3-5 days of crisis stabilization in a residential setting and approximately 20 days of follow-up outpatient services. While some health care providers offer lengthier terms of stay, few provide coverage of the long-term patient and family therapy that is necessary to rehabilitate the user.

In addition, the typical 12-step program (AA) is not well-suited for huffers. Inhalant users are often looked down upon by other drug addicts, and do not do well in a group therapy setting. Their thinking and concentration skills are greatly diminished by the damage of substance abuse. Experts recommend that inhalant users be treated separately.

"At the initiation of treatment, many users are lethargic, physically weakened and cognitively confused. Premature attempts to implement therapies that require energy and clarity of thought will only lead to failure and frustration, both on the part of the patient and the treatment staff," says Fred Beauvis in *Understanding the Inhalant User*. (Beauvais is a Senior Research Scientist at the Tri-Ethnic Center for Prevention Research at Colorado State University.) "Walking and talking sessions would probably result in the development of rapport and spawn greater conversation," says Mark Groves. "Action therapies such as art, music, drumming, dance and activities that involve hand-eye coordination need to be provided. These activities should be available during the day and evening hours so that inhalant users can positively channel energy when they experience the craving to sniff."

What's available?

Individuals who have the insurance to cover residential treatment still face many obstacles in finding facilities. Inhalant awareness among parents is almost nonexistent. A recent U.S. Consumer Product Safety Commission study showed that more than 95% of parents believe their child has never tried inhalants, compared with national statistics that show one in five (21.2%) eighth graders has used solvents in his or her lifetime. If parents do discover their child is a chronic huffer, it is difficult to find a treatment facility that has the expertise necessary to break the cycle of addiction. Many facilities will not accept inhalant users, while others put them through treatment modalities that are not suited for their needs. In Canada, there are a few treatment centers across the country and they have similar obstacles.

Users that enter treatment often do so through court directed programs. Accordingly, delinquent behavior—not inhalant abuse—can become the main focus of the therapy.

What can we do to stop the assault on our people?

- Become informed. Education is the key to preventing a child's deadly mistake. Educate yourself. Educate your family. Talk to your children about the dangers of Inhalant Abuse. If you contact the National Inhalant Prevention Coalition (In U.S.: 800-269-4237; In Canada call: 512-480-8953), they will send you a free video entitled "EDUCATE: Creating Inhalant Abuse Awareness Together."

- Contact your local officials to learn what programs they have which they have in place to educate and prevent solvent abuse. Support your local law enforcement officers in helping them stem the exploitation, abuse and killing.

- If you are a retailer, get a list of the solvents and refuse to sell them to anyone under 18. If necessary, ask for identification.

- If you live in an area where there are a lot of solvent abusers, get involved in the local outreach program to these broken people. A few churches have outreaches to solvent abusers and alcoholics. If there is no outreach in your area, consider starting one.

Sniffers are considered the lowest of the poor and outcasts, especially among our First Nations. Listen to them. Befriend them. Show them love and care; show that we are people who want them to find healing and wholeness.

In addition to funding more prevention and awareness efforts in schools and communities, private and government agencies should take action against inhalant abuse.

In order to fight inhalant addiction:

- more research on effective treatment is needed;
- therapists should be trained in appropriate treatment models;
- insurance companies should provide enough coverage to break the cycle of dependence; and,
- State/Provincial and Federal governments should be proactive in supporting prevention programs.

All who are involved should practice the three "Ps" of inhalant treatment—PREVENTION, PREVENTION, PREVENTION.

PERSONAL STORIES OF
THOSE RECOVERING FROM
SOLVENT ABUSE

I Hung Around With the Wrong Friends
by Malcolm

After years of drinking, sniffing, and crime, I wanted to get out. I hated my life. I wanted to get out of my home—get out of my family.

I never got much food at home and was hungry a lot of the time. I was always skinny. My family wasn't rich, though when I was younger, I wished they were. I wished I had a family that loved me and would hear my feelings, hurts and cries. I hated my family because they were drinking and abusive. I didn't like them.

My home was on a rough reserve in northern Manitoba. It wasn't a good experience to grow up on that reserve with all the drugs and alcohol.

I never had a relationship with my dad. I started drinking when I was 12 years old because I didn't feel I was accepted in the family or on the reserve. I was into violence and started hanging around with the wrong friends.

I started sniffing gas when I was ten or eleven years old. I sniffed gas for four years and drank for another two years. From the first time I sniffed, I knew I was addicted. It feels good the first time when you try it out.

Later on the next day when I got up, I knew I "needed more." The feeling that I got made me feel great at the time, but later I didn't know what I had done. If the police came to the door and said my name, I wouldn't know what I did the night before. I was tripping out—blackouts—like I just vanished from this earth or whatever. Your mind just goes crazy and you don't know what you did.

I started getting into gangs—thought I was cool. However, I felt like nothing was helping me out.

I was into Native spirituality and sweat lodges. I thought I would find healing there. Nothing helped. I was searching in the wrong places for help from the wrong people.

I thought my aunt would be able to help me and take me farther away from my family. I came down to southern Manitoba and started going to church. But I started getting into gasoline, drugs, and alcohol. Soon I was sniffing more than ever.

I thought no one loved me or cared for me. I kept going like that until one night, this lady had some friends in a home group come over to have a "fellowship." They were singing and praising God. I kept listening and this guy told me about Jesus, everything I hadn't heard about Jesus.

They were different. I told him to back off. I was scared. Going to my room I sat there for a while thinking. I came back out and sat on the couch. I was looking into this lady's and man's faces, wondering why they were so peaceful. There was a glow about them; they were different and I was searching.

This lady told me about Jesus. I asked, "Who's that?"

She answered, "Jesus is the Son that God brought down. He came down in the form of a man and shared the gospel with people like you—hurting people that suffered." She asked if I wanted to meet Him?

"I don't know who He is." But I was thinking that I wished I knew Him or could meet Him.

"He is here," she replied.

"Where is He? Is He a ghost or whatever?" I was freaking out.

"No," she answered, "No, He's in my heart and I'm happy."

I asked her why she was so happy and she said it was because of Jesus. I started crying. I was just searching for that peace.

"That's the peace you're looking for in your life," she said. "Your search has ended."

I took her aside and asked, "How can I get this peace or how can I find the love, whatever you've got in your heart?" I was crying and looking for something to cover my sins and pain.

"You've got to say a prayer," she told me.

"I don't know how."

"Just follow my prayer," she instructed. I followed her and accepted Jesus Christ as my Savior.

Since that night, I felt the hurts were lifted off my back. I felt like God said, "I'm here. Your search is ended. I'm the peace you're looking for."

I thought that with this Jesus I could get away from the drugs, gasoline and alcohol. I didn't know much about the Bible or that I was a child of God.

I stayed in that place for a year-and-a-half. Everything was going well. Slowly, my addictions were disappearing. Then I went back home. When I set my feet back on the reserve, I felt like Satan pulled me back home—like he said, "You're no good. Your friends are not here." I didn't feel that peace.

Everything came back again the night I got home: I was smoking, drinking, sniffing, and having girls. I started wondering how I could end this life. How can I get away from this thing?

I was going to hang myself one night. I felt like that was the way out for me. I had forgotten about God and everything they had taught me back there. I got into crime worse than before. The cops and people were looking for me.

When I felt I had nowhere else to turn, I asked my auntie to again help me out. She did and sent me back to the same place. This time I learned about Teen Challenge. They have a special treatment program for solvent abuse.

When I was 18, I entered into the program. I thought it was going to be one, two, three—quick! It was hard—it's not an easy walk. I thought God was saying, "It's not easy, Malcolm. You need Me…I'll be with you all the way, I'm going to help you."

I'm so thankful for this program. It's God through this program; it's only God, not these guys around here. The others with me in this program can't do anything if it wasn't for God in this program. I'm thankful that God opened this door for my life.

I'm not perfect yet until my Father calls me home. I'm not always strong. I have temptations as everyone does in this world. But I don't cover it with alcohol, sniff and drugs any more. I don't need to run to that. I run to God and ask for forgiveness; He's always there.

I don't want to go back to where I was. I want to keep on walking with the Lord. With His help, I plan to go back to school and after that whatever God wants me to do, whether that's going to Bible school to be a pastor or evangelist or whatever. I also want to go home and be with my family and just share how God has changed my life.

I Didn't Want to be Called "Chicken!"
by Kenny Lacquette

I started sniffing gasoline when I was nine. I'm 35 now, so that means I've been sniffing for almost 26 years. As I think back over my life, I see three reasons why I got into sniff and continued there. The first was peer pressure from my friends. Second, the miserable life I had as a child and teenager; and third, the example of my father.

Growing up on the reservation, I couldn't speak English until I came to Winnipeg when I was nine years old. At that age, I was sent to foster homes where I stayed until I was 13 and sent to the Portage Home for Boys.

When I was nine, I started sniffing gasoline. I was with my friends, my cousins, and my brother. They were sniffing that stuff. I said, "Let me try some."

They gave me a plastic bag and some gasoline and showed me how to "sniff." That first time I got quite sick. Then after that, because I wanted to hang around with them and be like them, I continued doing what they were doing.

I used to run away from home to sniff glue. It was easy to get the stuff. The older guys just got it for me and I paid them for it. I used to steal money from my home. Gasoline was free because we just siphoned it out of cars.

When I was ten I started drinking beer. I used to get drunk on three or four beers and I soon wanted more and more.

I wanted to be like my dad. My father had a lot of attention so I wanted to be like him.

One day I saw my dad drinking hairspray. He passed away in 1977 when I was 14. It hurt me a lot. After he died, I didn't care what I did or what happened to me.

Even when I was locked up, I did the stuff. I could get it in foster homes and group homes. I did it because I wanted to cure my problems, cure my hangovers. Sniffing helps you get over hangovers. It's better than an aspirin. After a while it got worse and I wanted more and more. To me, it was just like drinking water. I sniffed heavy every day, day and night.

I used to steal from my foster parents just to buy the stuff. My friends used to call me chicken and other names.

I said, "Okay then. I'll steal for you guys." I'd steal for them and I joined a gang, a little gang. We used to hang around together. There were 20 or 30 of us all together.

I lost a lot of my friends over the years. My cousin hung himself and two of my friends shot themselves in the head with a gun when they were all high.

Most of the time I didn't know what I was doing. I used to see things I never saw before when I was sniffing gasoline. I used to see images that weren't there. I saw aliens, monsters, people who seemed real, but weren't really there. I used to talk to them.

I went from gasoline to glue until I was 16 when I started using lacquer thinner. To me, it was all just like having another cigarette. You want more sniff.

By the time I was 15, I realized that I was addicted.

When I was 17, I was charged with first degree murder. I was involved in something with others that turned out to be murder. I was sentenced to two-and-a-half years in Stony Mountain (Manitoba) Penitentiary. From then until I was 25, I was locked up. Every time I got out, it wouldn't take long before I'd do some crime that'd get me arrested and back in the slammer.

During the years I was in prison, I started doing lots of drugs. I used to do marijuana, cocaine and needles. I got to the place where I'd shoot beer into my veins. That's how desperate I was. When I did that, I didn't care if I ever woke up.

All my life, if I wasn't locked up in foster homes, youth detention centers, or prison, I was on the street.

But in 1995, something happened that was the first step in turning my life around.

One day in October, I was walking down Main Street in Winnipeg, sniffing. A businessman pulled me off the street.

"Hey, come here."

I thought he was a cop. I replied, "Whadaya want?"

"Why don't you come tonight?" he answered.

"Where?" I asked, somewhat startled.

"Come to a barbeque."

I came for a barbeque of hot dogs and hamburgers and all the fixings. And it was free!

During the meal, John came up to me and said, "Kenny, you know what?"

Before I could respond, he continued, "I love you."

"You love me?"

"Yeah, and Jesus loves you too."

That was the first time somebody ever told me that he loved me. I thought white people hated me because I'm an Indian.

John invited me to come to their church. I did and I started learning that Jesus was there. After months of attending there regularly, I learned of my need of a Savior. I learned that Jesus was that Savior because He died to cover all the wrong things I had done in my life.

I accepted Jesus Christ into my life when I was 32. I started reading my Bible. I used to cry when I was alone in my room, tears running down my face. I used to pray,

"Lord, give me a good night's sleep tonight." And I would sleep well.

Shortly after that something happened that could only come from God. Three years ago, I had 18 charges of assaults, two counts of attempted murder, assault with a deadly weapon. My pastor and two young interns went with me to court.

"Ken," my pastor said, "you'll be lucky if you get less than three to five years for sure." While we were waiting to enter the courtroom, they prayed for me.

I figured I was going back to Stony Mountain. I prayed, "Lord, if you want me to go to jail, I'll go to jail."

When I sat in the court box, I felt somebody standing beside me. But there was no one there. It was like Jesus was standing there with me.

As the lawyer read the charges, 15 of them were dropped. Then the judge sentenced me to one year's probation, supervised by my church, and 80 hours of community service work. I couldn't believe it! It was a miracle!

Since that time, I've been going to different treatment centers. Most have not been good, because they do not include Bible teaching.

Since I've come to know Jesus, it's been a struggle. At first, I wanted my friends, but I also wanted Jesus. Satan was pulling one arm and Jesus was pulling the other and they were stretching me. I didn't know which one I wanted to go to. Finally, I said, "Forget it. I'm going with you, Lord. I'm going to come with you."

I went with the Lord and things started to happen. I started going to church regularly and hanging around people who love the Lord and who love me.

List of writers and contributors to the topic of Solvent/Inhalant Abuse:

Malcolm

Ken Lacquette

"Sniffing the Life Out of Shamattawa" by Shawn Ohler ©1998. *National Post,*
    November 23, 1998. Used with permission

© SYNERGIES 1997

CHAPTER EIGHT

Does Suicide

Still Call Your Name?

SUICIDE STATISTICS

- Once every 16 minutes someone commits suicide in North America.

- One person in 100 in the United States will die by suicide, and almost two people in 100 will die worldwide.

- One high school student in ten said that he or she had actually attempted suicide.

- There are more suicide attempts by girls and more completed suicides among men, by a ratio of almost three-to-four in the United States.

- Per capita, suicide rates are three times higher in Native North American communities as they are in non-native communities.

THE FIERCE GOOD-BYE:
HOPE IN THE WAKE OF SUICIDE

by G. Lloyd Carr and Gwendolyn C. Carr

Suicide is an ugly word, and the deed is an ugly deed. And there are some people who would say that "real Christians don't commit suicide." But the sad reality is that real Christians sometimes do; and Christian families and friends have to deal with the shame and guilt, as well as the grief and sense of loss and betrayal.

In the first few weeks after our daughter-in-law Kate's suicidal death, I found myself simply hanging on to God's promises that had helped me through those first days. Then as time passed and I gradually worked through my grief, I began to wonder about the whole issue. I knew about the Roman Catholic Church's teaching that suicide was "unforgivable" because there was no opportunity for repentance. But that idea did not fit with my understanding that Christ's sacrifice on the cross was enough to cover all sin.

And I remembered a part of Kate's last note where, in her deep despair and depression, she had written, "All I can ask is Christ's forgiveness and understanding ... I feel sick, sick at heart and tired of living ...[I] pray that Jesus will take me." Kate had asked for forgiveness. And I wondered how many other suicide victims have done the same thing.

I learned long ago that experience can teach us much, but I also learned long ago that any one person's experience is very limited. And so I turned, as I had done so many times before, to the Bible. As I studied it, I found some surprising things.

Suicide in the Bible

It usually comes as a surprise to know that there are so many suicides written about in the Bible. The one that probably comes to mind first is that of Judas Iscariot who betrayed Jesus to the Jewish leaders and then took his own life. Another one included in the New Testament is that of the jailer at Philippi who was getting ready to kill himself because he thought that his prisoners had escaped (Acts 16).

It is even more of a surprise to find out what the Bible writers say—and don't say—about suicide. In the Old Testament there are four clear cases of suicide. There is also a revenge killing in which a man dies along with the people he destroys. And there is one case which may be called a "mercy killing" (euthanasia), but which is usually considered a suicide.

One of the things we notice in the Bible is that when the suicide follows some military defeat or other terrible humiliation, and death or torture is certain, suicide is seen as "death with honor." In Judges 9, we read about a man named Abimelech who had been seriously wounded by a blow to the head by "a woman." For a soldier to die at the hands of a woman was considered a great disgrace. Trying to avoid the shame, and thinking that death would come soon anyhow, Abimelech took his own life.

A better known death in the Bible is that of Samson who, with his great strength, pulled away two central pillars on which a temple building stood (Judges 16). Samson's act is usually thought of as revenge on Israel's enemies, but it was really also a suicide. You will notice in Samson's prayer that he asks God for two things: (1) for enough strength to take revenge on the Philistines, and (2) to die.

And God answers both prayers. That may not mean that God necessarily approved of Samson's death wish, but it appears God gave help for the killing. It is interesting that even though he died by suicide, Samson is included in the Bible's list of "heroes of the faith" (Hebrews 11) who "of all, received divine approval."

There is also the suicide of Ahithophel, who had betrayed his king (2 Samuel 15,16). If he had waited, he would have been tried and executed as a traitor, his family disgraced, and their property taken away.

Instead he took care to return to his home, made sure all his affairs were taken care of, and only then took his life. By his action he provided for his family's future.

Suicide Burials

In the Bible, suicide victims are buried as other deaths. There is no evidence of the suicide victim's body being dishonoured or treated with lack of care. When the burial place is mentioned, it is in the family tomb if possible. The burials of Abimelech, Zimri, and Saul's armour-bearer are not described, but there is no evidence that their bodies were left unburied.

After King Saul's suicide, some loyal friends did what they could to give him and his sons a proper burial (1 Samuel 31). In Samson's case, his brothers and family retrieved his shattered body from the ruins of the Gaza temple and carried it forty miles to bury it in the family tomb (Judges 16). Concerning Judas, it is assumed that he was buried in "The Field of Blood," the field that was bought with the "blood-money" he had received for betraying Jesus. Later it was used as a burial ground for those who had no family tomb in Jerusalem.

In all these cases, the Bible does not seem to condemn the act of suicide itself. Neither do other history books of that time, such as the Mishnah and the Talmud which are the most important religious books for the Jews (other than the Old Testament).

Suicide is Not a Release

A book by Dietrich Bonhoeffer, a great German church leader who was executed by the Nazis in April 1945, speaks wisely about suicide. Bonhoeffer described suicide as "the self-accomplished expiation (payment) for a life that has failed" and the "attempt to give final human meaning to a life which has become humanly meaningless."[1]

Bonhoeffer knew much about suicide because many of his fellow prisoners resorted to suicide in the agony of the Nazi death-camps. Yet he counselled against that way of escape from misery. He believed that suicide is not the sin of murder, but the sin of lack of faith.

Since those dreadful days, survivors of the death-camps have told that it was those prisoners who kept their faith (either in themselves or in God) and who refused to give up in despair, were more likely to survive. But those who lost their faith were most likely to die. They felt that God had abandoned them in their time of trial and need, so they gave in to suicide.

Bonhoeffer taught that the "way out" of suicide is not a "release." He explained that lack of faith is so destructive because it hides a person from the truth. The truth is that even suicide cannot release a person from the hand of God, who has prepared his or her place for eternity.

Can We Say, "The Lord Has Taken"?

In the Old Testament we read about a man named Job. When Job had heard that he had lost all his children, his servants and all his possessions, he surrendered to God and said, "The Lord gave and Lord has taken away; blessed be the name of the Lord."

Often these words are spoken by Christians as they try to comfort people who are mourning the loss of a loved one. These words seem to make sense when there is death after an illness, death in a war, death by accident, or death through a violent crime. But can we dare say that about suicide: "The Lord has taken?"

This question is very real to someone who has lost a loved one through suicide. The same question can be asked about other losses too, and there is a very deep issue here. It has to do with people's freedom to make their own choices and with God's power to do exactly as He wishes.

On the one hand, there are people who believe so strongly in God's power to do His will that the individual person is really nothing more than a "puppet." At the other extreme are people who believe that natural causes and personal choices control everything.

The truth is somewhere in between. The Bible teaches that a person is responsible for his or her actions. The Bible also teaches that God is "sovereign" — He is in control of what people and nature do. And this is what makes it hard to understand. Somehow we must bring these two truths together.

We must say that the person who commits suicide is responsible for the act that took away life. But we must not say that, by that act, God's sovereign plan for the person was completely destroyed. To live with both these beliefs is difficult, but it must be done if we are to accept all of the Bible's teaching.

Yes, even when someone commits suicide we must say, "The Lord has taken." But no one who has had to cope with the pain of a loved one's suicide would believe that this is the right way to die. That pain is overwhelming.

The Last Enemy is Defeated

Suicide is about death, and death is the one thing that all people face for sure. There is much that the Bible can teach us about this. It begins in the first book of the Bible, in Genesis chapter 2 and 3. We read how the death penalty was given to the first man and woman, Adam and Eve. They had disobeyed God's command not to eat of the fruit of the tree of knowledge of good and evil.

The truth is that all of us, like them, have been disobedient to God (read Romans 5:12-14). As a result, death has come to us all. But even though death is the penalty of sin, and is called "the last enemy" (1 Corinthians 15:26), there is a positive side to death. It is the one guarantee that we will not have to live forever in a sin-cursed world.

Adam and Eve were kicked out of the garden especially to keep them from gaining access to the fruit of the tree of life (Genesis 3:22). If they had eaten from that tree as well, the hell of living forever in a sin-cursed world would be the only option for us all. But God in His mercy provided death, and that makes it possible to be saved! Yes, we must all die, but there is the promise of being raised up again. That is the hope of the gospel of Jesus Christ. The last enemy will be defeated!

God's Grace Here and Now

Though we as Christians look forward to being "raised up" someday, some of us must still live here and now with the pain of suicide. We personally have experienced the trauma of coming face to face with this kind of violent death. There are some who have had to discover the body, or had to identify a loved one in a hospital morgue. We have come home to an empty house and there was the feeling of grief and despair that almost overwhelmed us.

The *Dictionary of Medical Ethics* says that suicide "is the most significant of all deaths in its impact on the survivors."[2] Though those words are from a dictionary, we have felt them personally and strongly. We have sensed within ourselves the terrible loneliness and despair which drove our loved one to that last desperate act, and are horrified by it.

But there is still God's grace.

[1] Dietrich Bonhoeffer, Ethic, SCM Press, 1971, p. 142.
[2] Richard A. Fox, *Dictionary of Medical Ethics,* 1981, p. 426.
Adapted with permission from *The Fierce Goodbye: Hope in the Wake of Suicide,* G. Lloyd Carr and Gwendolyn C. Carr, Inter-Varsity Press, 1990.

SUICIDE EPIDEMIC:
THE TIP OF THE ICEBERG

by Gary Quequish

The headline read "Death stalks desperate reserve—suicide problem 'out of control.'" It is typical of the contemporary crisis faced by Native North Americans. I have had the grim task of doing funeral services for two nephews and a niece, along with two other boys from my village during the last five years.

The crisis of today's Native youth is only the tip of an iceberg of what is really happening in many villages. A news story from Regina, Saskatchewan gives light to what has happened to First Peoples. Two years ago, the city decided to do a project to determine if geese could be enticed to stay in the city for the winter. Heaters were installed in the lake to keep it from freezing. The geese did, in fact, remain for the winter, evidently thinking it was too warm to fly south. The following fall after the experiment was cancelled, the lake froze as usual. Alas, the geese stayed around after freeze-up. They refused to leave the frozen lake, and the city had to rescue them from perishing. They flew them south on a jet plane.

This is what I believe is happening to First Nations youth. They have been so conditioned to depend on the government for benefits that they have not been able to be and live on their own.

The Native American family unit has taken the greatest beating. Parents seem unable to parent for several reasons. The influence of Euro-Canadian culture has impacted northern communities in negative ways. The very fabric of their Indian culture has become disrupted. Parents are unable to relate to the "new" cultural values and changes. Worse yet, many parents struggle with the pain of their heart. Many attempt to drown their sorrows in alcohol and drugs.

Children are filled with shame because of treatment they receive from parents ranging from abandonment to sexual molestation. These youth carry a lot of hurts. Few parents know how to guide them through the difficult teenage years. This results in many turning to drugs, alcohol, sexual promiscuity and solvent abuse. These vices run rampant in our communities. Many children and youth carry enormous pain, despair, and are victimized beyond description.

Other changes are impacting Native Peoples in both positive and negative ways. Large corporate companies are raping the land of its resources, while providing badly needed employment for a few. Large hydro dams are built, destroying an entire way of life for numerous communities. Many fishing, hunting and trapping lands are permanently flooded.

Modernization of many communities has brought with it great socio-cultural upheaval. The healthy traditional values are disrupted resulting in the fracture of community structure. Geoffrey York comments on a western community that experienced just such an upheaval:

In the history of Canada, very few communities have ever been transformed from poverty to wealth so suddenly. As the oil money poured into Hobbema, the social upheaval was traumatic. Alcoholism increased, cocaine arrived on four reserves, families broke apart and the suicides mounted steadily...The oil money stripped them of self-respect and dignity...A culture can be destroyed as effectively by money as by disease or war. The influx of money...was an invasion by a foreign value system into a culture that had been based on hunting and fishing.

The disruption of the culture illustrated by Hobbema, Alberta is also true in many communities across Native North America.

In contrast to Hobbema, most Native communities are on the other end of the financial scale. Many communities are stuck in deep poverty with 90-95 percent unemployment, and social assistance is a way of life. Boredom ultimately leads to a crisis like that experienced by the Pikangikum, Manitoba community.

In the North there is also accessibility to various forms of media with minimal restrictions. Almost an entire generation has adopted Hollywood role models and the values that come with it. This has resulted in inmeasurable disillusionment and suffering.

There are other complex issues like the broken treaties, Indian Act, justice, land claims, and self-government. Racism and discrimination fed by centuries of stereotypes have resulted in deep ethnocentric attitudes on both sides.

The subject of contemporary realities must not close without at least a mention of life on a reservation. The total size of land set aside for national parks is five times larger than the total size of all reserve lands in Canada. Most houses in reserves are in need of major repairs. Homes are extremely crowded; many parents share a bedroom with their children. All of these are contributing factors that have disrupted the life of Native peoples. For many, the situation feels hopeless.

Former Grand Chief of the Assembly of First Nations, Ovide Mercredi, recalls the words of one Indian elder who had a vision:

> *He had a vision that of all us in Canada, including the First Nations, were entering a great rapids—a rapids no one has ever travelled before. No one knows the magic route to take. No one knows all the danger spots ahead, and there could be many. This is a journey I was told we must be part of. We must make the voyage together because we need each other. The Elder said our skills and knowledge will be needed in the turbulent waters ahead because we are experienced, having navigated many rapids in the past.* (Ovide Mercredi and Mary Ellen Turpel. *In the Rapids: Navigating the Future of First Nations.* Toronto: Viking Penguin Group, 1993, cover page.)

Help will not be found in Mercredi, the Elders, or any government political system. More programs will not curb the deep difficulties that exist in First Nations across this continent. A biblical writer of old reminds us:

> When I consider your heavens, and the work of your fingers, the moon and the stars, which you have set in place, what is man that you are mindful of him, the sun of man that you care for him?
>
> You made him a little lower than the heavenly beings and crowned him with glory and honor.
>
> You made him ruler over the works of your hands, you put everything under his feet.
>
> All flocks and herds, and beasts of the field, the birds of the air, and the fish of the sea, all that swim the paths of the seas.
>
> O Lord, our lord, how majestic is you name in all the earth!

God's original plan for man was much more than merely maintaining harmony in the lower world, physical world, other-than-human realm and the upper world of spirits. His plan was for man to bring Him glory and exercise a godly dominion over His creation; but, man chose to go his own way.

As mentioned earlier, the epidemic of suicides among our people was compared to the tip of an iceberg. Just as ships sink by striking the part of the iceberg that lies below the waterline, it is the "below the waterline" issues of communities and individuals that are sinking Native North Americans.

What a person does will always reflect who he believes he is in his heart. Compulsive drinking of alcohol, for example, is an outward expression of a deeper inner problem. A pattern has been set, and regardless of how hard a person tries to quit, he cannot get free. This way of managing life is rooted in painful experiences. The pursuit of relief is considered legitimate because of the pain.

These justified purposes are born out of the belief that this is how to avoid pain. Beliefs are developed from thinking in a certain way. In many cases, such as compulsive drinking, belief has developed into a strong vow. This vow has a lot to do with personal experiences of the past. These would be considered early memories of pain, shame, and trauma. All of these formulate a coping mechanism within a person's life, which, in later years, become a stronghold in which he is a prisoner.

The visible culture of an Indian (his customs and rituals) is connected to his internal view of reality. By maintaining harmony with the spirits he eventually forms a mode of worship in his heart. This mode of worship is compelled by a tremendous desire not to offend the spirits. In the context of these intense fears, deep-seated beliefs develop. The telling of legends conditions a Native person to think in a certain way about life in general. The trauma of fears experienced from early childhood causes an Indian to have a poor image of who he is as an Aboriginal.

Today, a Native American finds himself caught between his own Indian ways and the dominant white culture. His worldview is constantly changing. At times he wonders if he even has a worldview.

This confusion, however, only confirms the reality of our unique worldview. The current crisis among Native youth also reflects the uncertainty and frustration they are encountering. It would likely seem to an individual youth going through trauma that he has come to a place where he feels he has no place in the world. However, buried deep within his heart is a dignity that is damaged by life, but can never be destroyed. In the soul of every Indian is the capacity to believe in God and to embrace Jesus Christ as his Wounded Healer.

Interview with Phillip and Georgina Constant

Suicide is one of the most devastating tragedies to happen in any family or community. The pain that survivors are left with is beyond description. No one knows better than Phillip and Georgina Constant. They have not only lost their son through suicide, but also Phillip's brother as well as other relatives and friends. They are also involved in counseling survivors of suicide.

The following comments were compiled from an interview broadcast on Tribal Trails, a Native Canadian gospel TV program.

Tell us what led up to your son's suicide.

Georgina: Our son suffered from severe depression when he was 18 years old. He couldn't get out of bed, couldn't eat, and was just in bed sick. We finally had to commit him to a psyche ward.

During all of this time, we were going through a difficult struggle in our marriage. I was angry—angry at my husband, angry at my marriage and angry at God. It wasn't until later that I rededicated my life to the Lord.

At the time of my son's depression, my husband and I were separated. My son asked me to come home. It was in 1984. He said "Mom, please come home."

So I went back for him and in 1990 he committed suicide. When I was living away from the Lord, it was just like the Lord calling me back. Those words were ringing in my head and it was like the Lord said,

"Georgina, come back." So I did. I went back to the Lord.

How would you define depression?
Georgina: In the simplest words, depression is a lack of desire or interest in doing anything. My son enjoyed watching TV. It was one of his favorite activities. So when he quit watching TV—it was a clear sign something was wrong.

Phillip: When my brother was drinking heavy, that's another sign of depression, for adults anyway. Another form of depression is being sexually active (outside of marriage). People are trying to take the pain of depression away with different ways of doing it, but it doesn't go away.

How did your brother and son's deaths affect you, Phillip?
Phillip: At first, I tried to hide by drinking. It was basically the same thing my parents did. When something's hard, you set it aside and hope it'll go away, but it didn't go away.

When my brother committed suicide is when it really started to shake me up. One time in a hotel in Saskatoon, Saskatchewan, I realized that my heart was so cold, nothing was going to change, and nothing was going to make me move—just stone cold like it says in the Bible. That's where I was at that point. No one could come near me because of my anger—not because of the suicide, but because of my past life, my childhood.

My pain all started in my childhood. Being sexually abused, being abandoned and not having enough love and caring, and just not resolving these things about my childhood, brought me a lot of pain. I got married and took all these things with me—what my parents passed on to me. Then I passed it on to my boys. It's a long line of generational problems.

It's a difficult subject, but when was it that you finally started dealing with the fact that you were sexually abused?
Phillip: I kept it hidden for about 40 years. It's just recently that I brought it out. The Lord has opened up my mind, my memories. I always knew that they were there; I just had brushed them aside. I brought them out and began talking about them, giving them to the Lord and asking for forgiveness.

Also I began to see how much it had affected my marriage, my boys, my friends…everyone, and the anger began to disappear. God took that anger away.

I think it's so important for Native people to grieve. Grieving does not have to only involve death. There's grieving sexual abuse, abandonment, divorce. Every person has to deal with them.

Could you explain more about what you mean by forgiveness?
Phillip: I had to go back and forgive my mom and dad. I had to forgive myself. I had to forgive my sexual abuser. And I had to forgive everyone that hurt me. I had to deal with each one individually. It didn't just come in a list. It was a long process. People shouldn't expect sudden healing because, you know, one story takes a long time and there's so much pain in one story that you have to deal with them individually.

What part does denial play after a person commits suicide?

Georgina: A lot of denial. I couldn't accept it for a long time. Shortly after my son's death, our family counselor suggested that I start this group called "Survivors of Suicide." So my sister and I started that group right away in August of 1990. We had our first meeting in October 1990. I got involved a lot. We were invited to schools and communities to talk about suicide. My sister and I, we talked about suicide, and it still didn't phase me the way it should have. There was too much happening all at once.

In the span of twelve months my mother passed away, and a few months later, my son's best friend committed suicide, and then a few months later, he committed suicide...I was just in a total state of shock for a long time.

People used to say to me, "Oh, you're so strong, you know Georgina, you're so strong."

But I wasn't strong. I just didn't feel anything and I was like that pretty much for about a year. My way of denying it may sound silly to a lot of people. I made up this little story, I guess, in my head. I said to myself, "Oh those flying saucers, they must have come and got my son." That's what I said in my mind just so I didn't have to think about suicide.

Phillip: It's important for people that are grieving following a suicide, to know that there's such a thing as overload grieving and it's very strong. It could be spiritual too. So it's important for people to recognize it. Your body can only take so much and then denial comes into a person's life.

Often in suicide cases, there's a sense of loss of dignity. Can you address this?

Georgina: For me, I guess a lot of it is shame and anger. I remember this one incident where one of my sons said to me, "I hate it when people ask me" (even though I don't mind telling them). But as soon as I say "suicide," they look as if it's something weird, as if it's something to be ashamed of. Sometimes just the mention of the word "suicide" ends the conversation.

People don't know what to say; they don't know how to react. That in itself brings, especially in the beginning stages, a lot of shame and anger.

People handle suicide in different ways according to how or where they were at the time. For my husband, my son George and me, we were together at the time when we heard the news. Our other son, Craig, our youngest, was in The Pas at the time and he was there when all this was going on. Craig is handling it way differently than we are because we weren't there and he was.

It's a form of denial, but not really. I know that he is handling it in his own way, but it's still very hard to categorize the different ways that people deal with it because it affected my whole family differently.

How would you deal with someone who is depressed and struggling with suicidal thoughts?

Georgina: When a person is depressed or suicidal, they really need to talk to somebody; somebody they feel comfortable with. I've dealt with many people who are feeling suicidal and I get calls from parents who feel their child is suicidal. I try to get that person to talk about things that are bothering them. It may not be the real problem.

They'll say, "My girlfriend is leaving me," or something like that. They blame it on the present situation, but it's not that.

It's often something from the past that's bothering them, not the one they're distressed over at present. A lot of people make the mistake of having the wrong idea about suicide. That's where a lot of anger and bitterness come in too. If a boyfriend/girlfriend or even a husband and wife split up or they're having a lot of marriage problems and one of them commits suicide, people will blame it on the survivor. They don't understand that it's not their fault. It was something that happened to that person a long time ago—maybe that they even blocked out.

The more people that are involved, the better the chances a person has to survive these suicidal tendencies. In Proverbs 11:14 it says that "in a multitude of counselors, there is safety." The more people you get involved, the better the chances of getting that person through this depression.

Sometimes blame comes into play. People blame God; they blame themselves or they blame others. This seems the hardest thing to get over. How would you encourage people to get through this stage?

Georgina: There are stages in my life where I had to forgive my son for committing suicide. In a way it was always depressing and we always felt this danger of suicide so when he did do it, we had to deal with it for a long time and then I got to that point where I forgave him. I forgave him for committing suicide because, like I said, he wasn't well. Then I also had to forgive myself.

I knew that my son and I had a very close relationship. It was very, very special. Perhaps the hardest part was that my husband and son didn't get along and I blamed my husband too because they couldn't get along. I had to forgive my husband for that. I also had to tell God I was sorry for blaming Him for taking away my son and not making him well. I had a lot of forgiving to do. I wouldn't be able to function like I said unless I had forgiven. That is the key to freedom for me.

Phillip: There's one thing we always tell people that are having a hard time with forgiveness. It's easy to say to a person to give that pain to God—let Him have it. But it usually takes a long time for this person to realize what we are saying.

It's about forgiveness and when you finally give that forgiveness to God, then you can see the tears coming down because he's truly forgiven the pain that he's holding. By withholding forgiveness, he is destroying the life of the person. When that person finally gives it to God and says, "Lord, I'm giving it to you. I can't do anything more," that person will find that his life starts to change by forgiving. For my own life, that's how it has been.

What kind of things should people avoid saying or doing to a person who is thinking about taking his or her life?
Phillip: The most common mistake that people make is telling the person that "you'll go to hell." You know, that's

the last thing they care about. Or when you say, "Oh, things will get better." Little pat answers.

The thing to do is to sit down with that person and even make plans right then. Make out a schedule that will involve your being with that person. If it's in the morning, say, "We'll go for coffee at nine." I know I did that with one person. I said, "We'll go for coffee at nine o'clock tonight." When we went for coffee, I said, "We'll go for breakfast tomorrow." At breakfast the following morning I said, "We'll go to school and fill out applications." Just make daily plans. Keep the person going. At the same time, you're doing a lot of counseling. Everything you do is not a waste of time.

How important is the church to someone trying to recover?
Phillip: I think the church is the only way that you are going to heal. There's no other way. God is the only one that's going to heal you and your pain. It's important to realize that there are spiritual forces at work here and if those aren't met through prayer and counseling—if God isn't there, then you are not going to resolve anything. You're just going to get dragged deeper and deeper into whatever is bothering you and you have to have the Lord in you. That's where the healing comes from.
Georgina: It's very important for churches to be understanding about suicide. Church has an important role to play in dealing with the survivors of suicide. So many people have misconceptions about it. Many people's automatic response is, "Oh, the person went to hell." This reaction doesn't bring any healing. It only brings

out hate, anger and more bitterness and shame and blame.

Churches and people need to understand that suicide is something that needs to be looked at, not as a sin or as something that we can blame on someone or some system. There shouldn't be any more shame surrounding suicide because we have to trust that God knows what He is doing.

Is there anything that you want to add?
Phillip: We have a lot of pain and hide that pain from suicides. If a person is thinking about committing suicide, then talk to someone about it. Spare that grief to your survivors because it's a terrible grief. It's not something anyone should have to bear. It's so important to seek help. If you can't find anybody to help you, you have to be able to look further than where you're just staying at the moment. Don't just stay in this one dull spot and hope that help will come. Reach out.

Georgina: The best place is to turn to God. Pray. Pray for yourself and really do a lot of praying because God is there. Even if you feel that all your family has abandoned you, turn to God and He will bring the people into your life that will help you. Ask for those—ask for that help— the help will come. I know.

There are crisis lines you can call. Call a pastor, a friend, someone you may have met on the street. Go talk to somebody. Just pour it out.

HIGH RISK FACTORS

High risk factors are simply things that happen in the life of a person that make suicide a greater risk. We have to be on guard with the emotional (including mental and spiritual) and physical health of our youth. In order to identify sudden changes in a person's behavior, we have to know what their normal "patterns" are.

Listed below are a number of high risk factors, but this list is by no means complete or listed in any particular order.

- Has previously attempted suicide
- Is a victim of domestic violence, child abuse, rape or other assault
- Is a victim of incest
- Expresses a desire to die
- Is disconnected or alienated from family, community or culture
- Withdraws from family, friends, and teachers
- Is doing poorly in school
- Drops out of school or changes classes often
- Has known a family member or friend who has committed suicide
- Is involved with alcohol or drug abuse or has a family member involved with drug or alcohol abuse
- Suddenly appears peaceful during a crisis
- Leaves poems, diaries, drawings or letters to be found
- Expresses hopelessness, helplessness, worthlessness, and confusion

- Experiences a broken or difficult love affair
- Has family relationships that are falling apart
- Does not have a meaning or purpose in life
- Has no strength to tackle a problem and is blind to any way out

- *The use of alcohol or other drugs:* Alcohol is a depressant and people are often impulsive when using it. Over 70% of the suicides, deaths by automobile accidents, and violence takes place when people are drinking. After a heavy bout of drinking, a person is particularly high risk when they are sobering up/coming down and frequently feel guilty/shameful over some perceived, or real, transgression.

- *Victims of sexual abuse, especially incest:* Victims of sexual abuse feel "soiled" and feel they are not worthy, or feel they are at fault (guilty), even though they are the victims. Sexual abuse by parents or family members (incest) is very tragic. Sexual abuse by "authority" figures such as teachers, doctors, or pastors (priests) is particularly damaging. A sacred trust is broken and can rarely be repaired.

- *Has witnessed a suicide:* Witnessing a suicide, or even finding the body, is a terrible assault on the emotions. The person becomes a very high risk for committing suicide themselves. There is horror, shame, guilt and fear. They cannot get away from it. The image is carried within themselves. They experience trauma and are in shock.

CHECKING THE RIGHT BOX

by Raymond Dunton
as told to Kent Fraser

"Raymond, you're not white. You shouldn't mark that box," one of my coaches told me in front of the whole team. I was quite embarrassed and very angry when I went home.

My mom had always told me that when I was asked or had to fill out any papers, I needed to check the box that said I was white because I was Caucasian.

When I got home that day, I asked my mom why she had me mark the box 'white' when I really wasn't white.

My mother finally told me the truth. "You are Hopi and Navajo." She went on to explain that she didn't want for me to live with prejudice and rejection. And when I filled out an application for a job or anything else, she didn't want me to be passed by because I had marked some other box. She wanted me to have a fair chance of a job or a promotion and really just being treated fairly in life, in general.

In other words, my family was ashamed to be Indian. In fact, my mom wrote 'Caucasian' on my birth certificate.

When my grandparents relocated to Southern California and as I grew up, I was told that I was white. We lived in an area where there were many white people and in many cases I was the only one with dark skin. But I never thought anything of it and felt like I was just one of them. I continued to live with this understanding that

I was white until I got to junior high age. I knew what white looked like. And what I saw in the mirror certainly wasn't white so you can imagine I was pretty confused. But being a junior high kid, I asked my mom to explain why she insisted on that.

What really hurt me was for the first time in my life, I began being ashamed for being Indian. My mom and dad, my grandparents didn't feel it was good to be Indian so I felt that maybe a mistake was made somehow. That troubled me in my teenage years. I continued through my teen years and finally graduated from high school, still somewhat confused, thinking that I wasn't good enough. I was very conscious of my dark skin, always felt then that people were looking at me differently and maybe something was wrong with me. It caused me sometimes to try a little bit harder to be accepted and then when I didn't succeed I felt even worse.

Feelings Going Through My Mind

As I continued to experience confusion growing up, one of the things that added to that confusion in a very big way was the fact that I was sexually molested as a young boy. When I was abused by a couple of different men it began to confuse me as to why that happened.

Many feelings were going through my mind. When I became older, a teenager, I even began to question my sexuality. I was confused when it came to girls. I was confused when it came to other boys. I had heard people talk about homosexuality. I was confused and thought if I was touched that way by these men then maybe that meant that I'm was homosexual. I was scared because when I heard people talk about homosexuals it was in an unkind way. And so that caused me to become sexually involved with girls more to prove that I was not a homosexual.

These types of confusing thoughts ran through my mind on a daily basis. These were thoughts that I could not share with anybody and made me feel even lonelier. So I didn't experience a lot of peace, a lot of happiness, a lot of joy when I was growing up because of these different things I experienced.

One of the other ways that I tried to deal with the shame and embarrassment was to drink alcohol because when I drank alcohol I didn't have to feel the pain and shame.

My father, who was an alcoholic, would treat all of us kids very poorly. And it seemed like he picked on me more than the other kids and so that added to my shame and confusion. I found out later that when my mom was pregnant with me, my dad wanted her to have an abortion. And so as a teenager, living with that understanding too, I felt even more so that I was a mistake and that I wasn't wanted even by my own family.

Suicide Scared Me

One time my dad and I were having an argument and he told me I was crazy and I thought that was true. My dad told me I was so crazy that I would end up committing suicide. And that really startled me-really scared me.

Suicide scared me and I didn't know what to think of that so I didn't say anything.

My dad continued to yell at me. "And you want to know the funny thing about it?" And I thought to myself "How can there be a funny part of suicide?"

"What? What's the funny part about that?"

"I'm the one who's going to hand you the gun," he replied.

From then on I was very fearful of my dad and very fearful of guns. I lived the rest of my teenage years in confusion and fear always wondering when would be the day my dad's "prophecy" would come true and he would hand me a gun and yell, "Do it!"

When I finally graduated and left home I still had those thoughts running through my head. I continued to use alcohol even though I saw how it ruined my family. It was the only time I found any type of relief from the fear, thinking that I might kill myself because I was crazy. The way that I could deaden the pain of the hurt because I wasn't even wanted and should have been killed when I was still inside my mother. And the fact that I was Indian and it wasn't a good thing to be Indian. These were things that filled my life.

It eventually caught up with me, this whole use of alcohol and the lifestyle of drugs and immorality. I had to spend some time in the Los Angeles county jail. When I was in jail I got to thinking about a lot of things and evaluating my life. Of course I had to remain sober and I didn't have access to drugs. I was just thinking about life in general and it really wasn't pleasant for me. It seemed hopeless. It seemed very lonely. I really had more questions in my head than answers and that frightened me.

So I started thinking about why I was in jail. I really didn't blame anybody else for my being there because I knew I was in there for the choices that I made. Nobody forced me to make the choices that I did in life. I did them on my own.

Toward the end of my jail term, the thought came to mind "Well, the only way I'm going to be able to make some change is for something that is much more powerful, something that is much bigger than me in order to make that change." Then the thought came, "Maybe what I need is God."I didn't know where to find God. I didn't grow up understanding the traditions and the religion of my people, the Hopi people and the Navajo people. Nor did I grow up in a home that exercised or practiced any type of religion. So I didn't know where to look for God. I knew where to find alcohol, drugs and sex. But I didn't know where to find God. I didn't know how to go about using God for a change to take place in my life.

The time came for me to leave jail and I was still thinking about God. How do you go about having God change your life for the good?

When I got home to my apartment my roommate, who was originally from Minnesota, had just come home from a job trip and he wanted to share some exciting news with me. Well, first I told him I had to tell him about my news--of being in jail.

After telling him he said, "Let me tell you what happened to me." While he was in northern California he met some people who talked to him about God.

They shared with him from a piece of paper how he could have God in his life. He told me that he now had a relationship with God.

"Tell me," I replied with a sense of jealousy in my voice. "Tell me, too, how I can have God in my life because I need changes."

Well, my roommate was very tired because he had been traveling on the road for over twelve hours so he told that he needed some rest before he could share that news with me. I was very disappointed. In fact, I was thinking in my mind, "What if he dies in his sleep? Then I will never know." Then I thought, "What if, while he is sleeping he falls out of bed and he bumps his head and he loses his memory?" These crazy thoughts kept coming into my mind because I was very anxious and I wanted to know how I could invite

God to be a part of my life in a very real and personal way-so that personal changes could take place. I knew I needed help and I knew that I needed help from God.

'You don't understand'

Finally, my roommate woke up. By the way, he didn't lose his memory and he didn't die in his sleep. So he was willing to talk to me and share with me what he had learned.

And when it came time for me to pray to receive God's plan for my life through His Son, I said to my roommate "I can't do that now. I can't pray that now."

"Why not, Raymond?" my roommate asked me.

"You don't understand. There are a lot of things in my life that I need to fix first. I need to stop drinking and taking drugs. I need to stop messing around with women. I need to clean up my life before I'm ready for God; before God is even willing to accept me." And then I explained a little bit further to him.

I tried to use an illustration because he didn't understand what I was saying.

"You have given me the plans to build this boat," I told him. "This boat represents a new life with God and what I need to do is piece by piece put it together. And once it's completed, then I'll be ready and then God will be ready for me to come aboard this boat and to sail along this new life with him."

Al looked at me and said, "Raymond, you're the one that doesn't understand.

God has already built that boat for you and that boat is His Son. You just need to be willing to accept that. Make the choice to receive it and come on board the boat and allow God to sail this new life for you."

"I like that. I like that plan," I told Al.

I prayed at that moment and invited God into my life and I began to realize and really truly understand that I was not a mistake. God knew before all of creation that I was going to be born Indian. And He knew before creation that I would go through some pain and confusion.

Even though it was not part of His plan because His plan is a good plan and a perfect plan, He is a good God, a caring God and a loving God. And then I began to understand God didn't make a mistake when He made me Indian.

He made me Indian because He's proud of me and He wants me to stay Indian.

And He's glad now that I am His child. I have received His Son into my life and have become part of His family and God is happy and pleased when all Native American people come to Him for help.

No More Fear

We can not make a good change in our lives without Him. I began to read God's book, the Bible, He explains not only His story and what good plans He has for His people but there are also instructions there. There is also a message of hope and that how we can live a life through His strength. It took a little bit of time-not a long time-and I was free from alcohol, from drugs and I was free from sexual immorality.

I no longer lived in fear. I no longer was angry and bitter at Mom and Dad or my grandparents. I forgave them. I was finally able to forgive them because I understood that God had forgiven me and forgiven them also. And so we are told that we must forgive others as God has forgiven us.

I love my family and I want to introduce them to God so they too don't have to be ashamed and live in fear. This is my desire to share this message of hope with everybody I come in contact with. You have an opportunity to receive this hope, to have a personal relationship with God the Creator.

You don't have to live in fear. You don't have to live with alcohol and drugs. You don't have to live with the lie thinking that you are a mistake.

God loves you and there is an opportunity for you to experience that love because He gives that love to everybody who is willing to receive it.

FACTS ABOUT SUICIDE

Four out of five people who commit suicide have talked about it or threatened it previously. It is a myth that someone who talks about it won't do it. Most often that is a very clear call for help.

Drugs or alcohol are involved in two-out-of-three suicides.

A suicidal person is not necessarily mentally ill. He or she may be simply seeing things through a very distorted and constricted lens—there seems to be only two choices for this individual: continuing to have a powerful sense of pain, or that pain stopping.

The act of suicide is not seen as a moving toward something, but as a moving away from an unbearable pain. Most suicidal people are undecided about living or dying. Happily, most are suicidal for only a limited time and, if saved from self-destruction, go on to lead useful lives.

Some Warning Signs to Look For:

- Sleeplessness
- Unable to concentrate
- Anorexia
- Weight loss
- No energy or very active
- No desire to socialize
- Seems withdrawn
- Seems preoccupied
- Often appears bored
- Gets upset easily

- Poor personal hygiene
- Crying
- Feeling worthless
- Appears sad

Things a Suicidal Person May Say:
- "I'm going to kill myself!"
- "I wish I were dead!"
- "The only way out is for me to die."
- "I just can't go on any longer."
- "You're going to regret how you've treated me."
- "I'm so lonely."
- "Life has lost its meaning for me!"
- "Nobody needs me anymore."
- "I'm getting out of here."
- "Here, take this (valued possession); I won't be needing it anymore."

THE OWLS SPOKE NAVAJO
by Pete Grey Eyes

If you were to fly like a bird across the Arizona landscape, you'd see dry, rough scenery—the desert. It's a wonder that much of anything can grow in that wasteland. Yet, a closer look will reveal that it is teeming with life.

In a way, that's a lot like my life. For much of my life, there was a dryness. My life was dead in many ways. But something happened about 20 years ago which brought life to my soul.

I was born in 1927 into the home of Earl Grey Eyes, a Navajo medicine man and shepherd in the traditional way. Life was not easy. From the time I was very small I learned to shepherd the sheep, taking them from one grazing place to the next and watching over them as only Navajo shepherds can.

I received my schooling at the feet of my father who not only taught me the Navajo ways, but also the ways of the medicine men.

At the age of 14, I left home to work on the railroad. During World War II many Navajo worked on the railroads. It was my job to see that the cooking supplies, bunks, and housing facilities were moved from site to site. My work took me to several western states including Colorado, Utah, Washington, California, and New Mexico.

After several years on the railroad, I returned to Navajo Mountain, Arizona, to take up farming and raise livestock. I also followed in the footsteps of my father and became a medicine man.

For many years I practiced my medicine. I treated many people. I had great power and control over the people in the surrounding area. My reputation was soon well known. I had great influence.

Something Strange and Terrible

But something strange and terrible began to happen in 1974. A couple of people from the Alliance church began visiting us every so often to share with us the message of Jesus. My wife was interested, but I didn't want anything to do with them.

Then my family became sick. My wife was very sick. I tried all my potions and powers, but nothing did any good. We took her to the hospital in Gallup, New Mexico and then to Albuquerque. The doctors said there was nothing they could do for her.

Then my three daughters became ill. I also fell sick to this unknown illness.

Something strange began to happen. My sheep, cattle and horses began to die for no reason at all. Then other things began. Coyotes started coming around our place at night and howl. This is a very bad sign for us Navajo.

Then, worst of all, owls began to appear in the juniper trees outside our hogan. There was not only one but several. They would come and hoot throughout the night.

As time went on, these owls began to talk to me in a Navajo way. They would say, "We are going to kill you…you…you! We are going to kill you!"

I knew these owls weren't speaking to me themselves. They were demons sent by another medicine man to an owl. When a medicine man makes contact with the spirit world, these spirits are given to him to help him in his dealings in witchcraft. A medicine man could use these demons and send a demon in an owl to a certain family and pester them and eventually this fear will kill them as time goes on. This is what was happening to me and my family.

I tried all my powers to get rid of these owls and stop my livestock from dying and to heal my family, but nothing changed. It was no use!

My wife got worse and she was taken to Albuquerque. They sent her home to die.

After trying everything, I realized that perhaps the Christian friends who had been visiting us had an answer. It was my last—maybe my only chance—for survival.

That evening I took my wife and three daughters to church. It was rather late when we arrived and the church was packed. The only place to sit was on the front row. They ushered us down to the front.

I Needed an Answer

There seemed to be a hush fall over the place when we walked in. I guess most of those attending never expected to see the medicine man and his family in church!

The preacher, a man by the name of Herman Williams, was just about finished his message. It seemed like right away he asked if there was anyone who wanted to turn his life over to God.

I didn't understand it all, but I knew that I needed an answer and if this preacher said Jesus was the answer, that's what I needed.

Right away I was on my feet. My wife and daughters followed me. We knelt together in front of the altar.

The church had people right there to take us into side rooms to counsel with us.

"What is it you want God to do for you tonight?" they asked me.

I told them that I had come to the end of my rope. I explained how my livestock was dying for no reason and my family was sick. I told them about the owls and the coyotes.

"I have come tonight because I know that God is the only only who can help me out of this terrible situation," I said. "I want to accept Him as my Lord and Master. I've come for salvation and for healing."

Child of Light

Together they led me in a prayer asking Jesus Christ to come into my life and forgive me for all the terrible wrongs I had done. Right then and there God changed my life. I didn't understand it all, but I knew I was no longer a child of darkness, but a child of the Light.

When I had finished praying, we came back and I rejoined my wife and daughters in front. They asked us to share what had happened.

My wife was first. She told how she had been very sick. How the doctors had sent her home saying there was nothing they could do for her.

"Tonight," she said, "I have accepted the great medicine man (great physician in Navajo) to save me and make me well."

Then my three daughters joined in and spoke of how they had committed their lives to Christ. Then it was my turn to speak.

"You people all know me as the medicine man of this area. Many of you have called upon me and I have doctored you. But my wife has been very sick. We have all been sick. I tried everything in my power to doctor my wife, my children and myself. But things have gotten worse. Our sheep are dying; our cattle and horses. Other things are bothering us.

I'm glad that I came to make my commitment to the Lord Jesus Christ."

When we were finished, the whole church stood and they each took turns greeting us and offering us words of encouragement.

I spoke with Herman Williams before we left the church that night and asked if I could speak to him about something. He said sure so I shared with him the problem I'd been having with the owls and coyotes.

"How can I get rid of those owls?" I asked Pastor Williams.

He thought for a moment and then he said, "They can talk to you so they must understand you. So this is what you need to do tonight. When you get home, you will probably see those owls there. I want you to give your testimony to them of what happened to you tonight."

We didn't get home until about three o'clock in the morning. Sure enough, the owls were there. I could see them sitting in the juniper trees.

I nervously cleared my throat and began to speak to these birds.

"You owl people, I have something to tell you. When we left last evening, we went across to a church. We heard a message about a Savior, the Lord Jesus. We have all committed our lives to Him—myself, my wife, and our three daughters."

I continued to tell them my testimony. "I gave what sheep I have, what cattle and horses I have to the Lord. My home and my dogs and cats. Even this grazing territory I gave to the Lord.

"You all are trespassing, every one of you. In the name of this Great Chief, the Lord Jesus Christ, I command you, every one of you to leave our place and never come back, in the name of Jesus."

When I stopped, it was so quiet I could have heard a pin drop. Dead silence.

I began to wonder if they heard me. Then way in the back an owl took off. Then another. And another. One right after the other until they were all gone.

To this very day, over twenty-two years later, they have not come back.

You know, the Lord Jesus is not only the Savior of the world, He is also the Great Physician. He brought healing and freedom to my family.

We found out later that there were five medicine men who had put curses on my family and everything I owned. Praise God His power is greater than that of any medicine man. Through the precious blood of Jesus my family and I found true freedom and life.

Pete Grey Eyes is a pastor with the Christian and Missionary Alliance on the Navajo Reservation in Arizona.

DOES THE OWL STILL
CALL YOUR NAME?

Are you still struggling with one of the addictions covered in this book? Would you like to have peace and freedom in your life? Would you like to be able to command those owls to leave you and never return? You can but you can't do it on your own. You need the Creator's help. That's why He sent His Son to live among us and to die in order to become the sacrifice for our wrongdoing.

The Creator's Son Jesus wants to come into your life, forgive your sins and give you hope and healing. Here's how to ask him into your life:

- Tell God that you want to accept His way to know true peace and joy.

- Tell Him that you know that without His help, you will be separated from Him in life and in death.

- Accept Jesus as God's only provision to deal with your separation from Him.

- Invite Jesus to take control of your life and place you in His care.

Pray this prayer (or use your own words):

> *Dear God, I accept Your way. I believe Your Son Jesus died for my sins so I could become part of the family of God. Because You raised Jesus*

from the dead, I can now experience "Harmony of Life" with Your Son as my Shepherd. I tell you I'm sorry and turn from my sins and ask You, God, to take charge of my life. I offer this prayer to You through Your Son, Jesus. Amen.

Christ came to set us free (John 8:32,36). He has also promised to rescue us someday from the pain of this present life (Revelation 21:4). Until that day comes, He has promised to help us by His presence in the midst of despair.

"Even if I walk through the valley of the shadow of death, I will not be afraid of anything, because You are with me. You have a walking stick with which to guide and one with which to help. These comfort me" (Psalm 23:4).

If you have prayed the prayer above, we would like to hear from you. Fill out the coupon and mail it to:

In the United States:
Indian Life Books
P.O. Box 32
Pembina, ND 58271

In Canada:
Indian Life Books
P.O. Box 3765, Redwood Post Office
Winnipeg, MB R2W 3R6

NAME _____

ADDRESS _____

TOWN/CITY _____

STATE/PROVINCE _____

ZIP/POSTAL _____

If you would rather not cut up this book, you can write to us on a separate sheet of paper. We have some helpful information we'd like to send to you.

"Does the Owl
Still Call Your Name?"

More Good Reading

Indian Life

Indian Life is one of the most widely read Aboriginal publications in North America. In its pages you will find positive news of Indian people and events, first-person stories, photo features, family life articles, and much more. Published six times a year. Write for a free sample copy. Find out why almost 100,000 people read this newspaper.

The Conquering Indian

An amazing collection of 70 stories showing that Jesus Christ can heal the deepest hurt of Native people. This book tells the stories of how these people, young and old, reached out to Jesus and how He answered their pleas and helped them to have victory over the problems and conquer them. This book can be used to guide you to the One who can help you win that victory. 332 pages.

The Grieving Indian

Every Native person needs to read this book for the help and hope it offers. With over 70,000 books in print, find out why it has attracted so much attention.

Read one man's story of pain and hopelessness. Learn how his wife took a desperate step to turn his life around. This is a powerful book of hope and healing. 128 pages

Whiteman's Gospel

"This is one book that should be read by every man and woman in North America," says Bill McCartney, founder of Promise Keepers. The author, Craig Stephen Smith, Chippewa, examines Christianity and how it has affected Native Americans. His experience has led him to believe that change is desperately needed in both native and church communities. 154 pages

The Council Speaks: Answers to questions Native North Americans are asking

Over the last 20 years, Indian Life newspaper has published a column of questions readers have asked. A Native North American council has answered questions on life, tradition, culture, and practical issues. These may have been questions you have had, but were afraid to ask. Join the circle and listen to the answers. It may change your life! 122 pages

VIDEO:

Learning to Fly: The Path of Biblical Discipleship

A true to life story that illustrates the challenges of a new believer. This video will change your life and the life of your church by giving you a perspective on what discipleship is all about. It will show you why making disciples is so important. The Great Commission is more than making converts—it's making disciples. That's done through relationship.

For prices and to order the above products please call Indian Life Books at 1-800-665-9275 or write:

In the U.S.
Indian Life Books
P.O. Box 32,
Pembina, ND 58271

In Canada:
Indian Life Books
P.O. Box 3765, Redwood Post Office
Winnipeg MB R2W 3R6

If you are still struggling with one or more of the issues dealt with in this book, here are some resources where you can find help.

There is help for those who are hurting

Sexual Brokenness:

If you are HIV positive, suffering with AIDS, or you're struggling with homosexuality, here are some groups you can contact for help and information:

WHERE GRACE ABOUNDS
PO Box 18871
Denver, CO 8028-0871
Telephone: 303-863-7757

WHERE GRACE ABOUNDS is a Christian ministry formed to help men and women who are in conflict with their homosexual behavior and want support and guidance to change. They reach out in the love of Jesus Christ without condemnation yet without compromising the Word of God. They offer individual counseling, counseling through letters, support groups, literature and seminars. They also provide information on AIDS.

LOVE & ACTION
3 Church Circle
Annapolis, MD 21401-1933
Telephone: 1-800-947-9500

Working along with hospital workers and social workers, LOVE & ACTION is ministering to the material, emotional and spiritual needs of AIDS patients. Through the distribution of personal care items, as well as Christian literature and music, the staff is able to bring comfort and hope to those who are sometimes deserted by friends and relatives.

NEW DIRECTION FOR LIFE MINISTRIES
Box 1078, Station F
Toronto, ON M4Y 2T7
Telephone: 416-921-6557

Alcoholism:

ALCOHOLICS ANONYMOUS (AA)

– located in many places in North America. See telephone directory.

TEEN CHALLENGE

– located in many places in North America. See telephone directory.

Child Abuse:

IN THE U.S.:
CHILDHELP USA National Headquarters
15757 N. 78th Street
Scottsdale AZ 85260

Telephone: 480-922-8212
Child Abuse Hotline: 1-800-4-A-CHILD
(1-800-422-4453)
In Canada:
The Canadian Society for the Investigation of
Child Abuse
P.O. Box 42066
Acadia Postal Outlet
Calgary, AB T2J 7A6
Phone: 1-403-289-8385
Email: info@csica.zener.com

FAS/E

In Canada:
FAS/E Information Service
75 Albert Street, Suite 300
Ottawa, ON K1P 5E7
(800) 559-4514

In the United States:
Indian Health Service, Headquarters West
Fetal Alcohol Syndrome Project
5300 Homestead Road N.E.
Albuquerque, NM 87110
(505) 837-4228

NATIONAL INFORMATION CENTER
FOR CHILDREN AND YOUTH WITH
DISABILITIES (NICHCY)
PO Box 1492
Washington, D.C. 20013-1492
(202) 884-8200 or 1-800-695-0285

Gambling:

Are you a gambling addict and want help to be free?
There is help. Please contact the following programs:

FREEDOM IN CHRIST MINISTRIES
In the U.S.: 1-866-462-4747
In Canada: 1-306-546-2522

Contact either of these numbers and they will help
you find the counseling program nearest you. After
contacting the above agencies, if you still need help,
please contact us and ask to speak with someone about
gambling. Our number is: 1-800-665-9275.

Pornography:

NATIONAL COALITION FOR THE
PROTECTION OF CHILDREN AND FAMILIES
800 Compton Road, Suite #9224
Cincinati, OH 45231
513-521-6227
Victims' Assistance HelpLine 800-583-2964

FOCUS ON THE FAMILY
8605 Explorer Drive
Colorado Springs, CO 80920
(719) 531-3400

Solvent/Inhalant Abuse:

If you or someone you know is seeking help for inhalant
abuse, you can contact the National Inhalant Prevention
Coalition at 1-800-269-4237 for information on treatment centers and general information on inhalants.
Through a network of nationwide contacts, NIPC can
help (but not guarantee) finding a center in your area that
treats inhalant use. They will send a free video entitled
"EDUCATE: Creating Inhalant Abuse Awareness
Together."

Where you can make contact:

In the U.S.:
National Inhalant Prevention Coalition
1201 W. Sixth Street, Suite C-200
Austin, Texas 78703
Phone: 1-800-2694237

In Canada:
1-512-480-8953

If you are able to access the Internet, you can look at
the NIPC website at: www.inhalants.org

You can also contact:

In the U.S.:

National Drug and Alcohol Treatment Referral Service

1-800-662-HELP

National Clearinghouse for Alcohol and Drug Information

1-800-729-6686

Suicide:

Suicide Crisis Lines

If you are discouraged or depressed and feeling like life is not worth living, there is someone who wants to talk to you. Listed in the front of your telephone directory are crisis telephone numbers. If you can't find any, call the number below.

We regret that space doesn't allow us to include numbers in every state or province. By calling the toll-free number below, they will give you the crisis number nearest where you live. Please don't hesitate. Call now.

1-800-999-9999